Hot Chocolate
With God 2

Camryn Kelly

with Jill and  Erin Kelly

Hot Chocolate With God²

Just Me & My Friends and Family

FaithWords

New York   Boston   Nashville

All Scripture quotations, unless otherwise indicated, are taken from the *Holy Bible,
New International Version®. NIV®.* Copyright © 1973, 1978, 1984 by Biblica, Inc™. Used
by permission of Zondervan. All rights reserved.

Scripture quotations marked (NLT) are taken from the *Holy Bible, New Living
Translation*, copyright © 1996, 2004, 2007 by Tyndale House Foundation. Used by
permission of Tyndale House Publishers, Inc., Carol Stream, Illinois 60188. All rights
reserved.

Definitions quoted in the text are from the *New Oxford American Dictionary.*

FaithWords
Hachette Book Group
237 Park Avenue
New York, NY 10017

www.faithwords.com

Printed in the United States of America

CWM

First Edition: September 2012
10 9 8 7 6 5 4 3 2 1

FaithWords is a division of Hachette Book Group, Inc.
The FaithWords name and logo are trademarks of Hachette Book Group, Inc.

The Hachette Speakers Bureau provides a wide range of authors for speaking events.
To find out more, go to www.hachettespeakersbureau.com or call (866) 376-6591.

The publisher is not responsible for websites (or their content) that are not owned by
the publisher.

Library of Congress Cataloging-in-Publication Data
Kelly, Camryn, 1999–
Hot Chocolate with God. #2 : just me and my friends and family / Camryn Kelly with
Jill and Erin Kelly. — First edition.
pages cm
ISBN 978-0-89296-844-2
1. Christian life—Juvenile literature. 2. Girls—Religious life—Juvenile literature. I. Kelly,
Jill, 1969– II. Kelly, Erin, 1995– III. Title.
BV4551.3.K43 2012
248.8'2—dc23
2011048037

This amazing book is

dedicated to girls . . . like

you.

Girls loved by an awesome,

incredible GOD!

Girls created ON

PURPOSE to

LIVE, LOVE, and LAUGH!

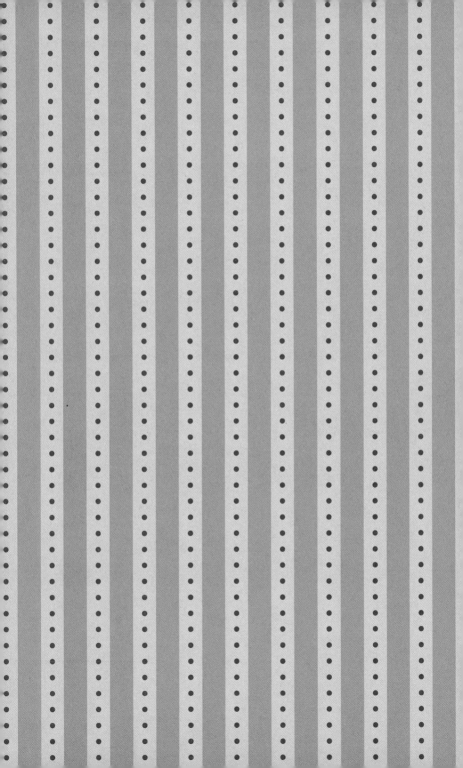

This
sensationally sweet
book belongs to:

· ·

Do not let anyone look down on you
because you are young, but set an
example for the believers in speech, in
life, in love, in faith and in purity.

I Timothy 4:12

Thank you . . .

Bailey and Kiley Rush—Can you believe it . . . *HCWG* #2! You rock! Thank you for your help and for making me laugh out loud all the time.

Ally Curtin—Girl, we love you! Thanks for the video and creative fun! You're the best!

Kim and Paige Waggoner—Aunt Kim and Paige, I love you both! *The Hot Chocolate with God* book series is great because of you. Thank you for praying!

Patti Thomas—You're so funny. Thank you for all your help. Love you always.

Rick Kern—I'll always remember how much you have helped us succeed! Thank you for everything.

The FaithWords team—Jana, this book would not be what it is without you and your team. We love you and thank God for you.

Team Wolgemuth—Thank you for supporting my writing. I'm so grateful for you.

To my mom and sister, Erin—We did it! *Again!* God is so awesome! I love you more than words can say!

Finally, to Jesus—I'm Yours! Thank you for loving me and for showing me that You are always there for me. I trust You to use this book to help girls know You more. You're amazing!

Contents

First Things First . . .

Here's the deal—this is not just another book. If you've already read my first book, **Hot Chocolate with God—Just Me and Who God Created Me To Be**, you know this is way more than a book. (If you did read it—NICE. I wish I could hug or high-five you right now. If you haven't read it yet, don't wait, girl. Go get it, or connect with me through the website **www .hotchocolatewithgod.com** and I'll make sure you get a copy.)

This book, the one you're holding right now, is you. It's about who you are right now and who God is creating you to be! It's your life journey.

With me!

Yes, with me! I'm hoping that if I share my heart and hope with you, you'll share your life with me. I wish we could actually hang out, but since we might not ever meet in person, I'm hoping we can get to know each other here and on the **Hot Chocolate with God** website (which is pretty much the hottest spot to hang out on the Internet for girls like us).

I've grown up some since the writing of the first book and I guess you could say I'm a little bit wiser now (and more hysterical). So I have more to share with you this time. More funny stories to crack you up. More epic videos. More sharing of my real self—my heart. It's not always easy to share your real self with total strangers, but I believe God wants us to know each other. More important, God wants us to know Him.

So, this book is a fun, fresh way for us to get to know each other. It's also an easy and creative way for you to share your life and the great things God is doing in your heart even now. But better than all that, I really think this book journey will change your life. I'm not exactly sure how, but I hope and pray that God will bless and encourage you through **Hot Chocolate with God**. I believe that you will discover more about yourself, your friends and family, and the God who created you through these pages. Because the truth is, He loves you like crazy, more than you can understand. He has a plan in all of this and it's good—better than you and I can possibly imagine.

Are you ready?

If you know me, you know that I already have my purple sparkly pen all set to go. (Well, not in my hand right now because I wouldn't be able to type this book if I did . . . hee-hee.) You need to grab a cool pen too, and not a boring black or blue one if you can help it. I know where to get the best pens ever. We'll get to the cool pen discussion later.

Let's go! Or as my sister, Erin, would say "Leggo."

I'm so excited!

Thanks for being right here, in the midst of these pages with me.

With love and a heart full of life,

Camryn ("Cam")

P.S. Let's rock this!

FYI, Before You Go Any Further

Before you get started, you should probably read this page. (Seriously, this is the page that I always skip over when I'm reading a book, but don't do it. I would like you to know a few things before we roll on, okay?)

1. This book is yours! What you write in here, stays here. This is your space to share how you feel and say what you want. A special place to be you. I've organized this book into **Sweet Sections**, but you can read it in whatever order you want. I suggest moving from section to section, but if that's not your thing, flip through and start wherever. And remember—have FUN!

2. In case you haven't figured it out yet, I go by my nickname, Cam. You'll find *Cam Jam* here and there as you read through this book. This is where I have decided to share my heart and life with you. I'm me, and I hope that being honest and open with you will encourage you to do the same. Besides, girl, God made you. He has a plan for your life! He has a plan for my life. So let's just be ourselves and do this, party up together.

3. Going on the Internet just got more fun! We have a website! A website just for YOU! Thank God! Throughout this book I will invite you to go and check out the **Hot Chocolate with God** website

(**www.hotchocolatewithgod.com**) to view 🎥 **Cam Clips**. We've had a blast creating these videos. Although I will admit it was a lot of work too. When you see a 🎥 **Cam Clip**, there will be a special code word next to it that you will need. When you go to the 🎥 **Cam Clips** section on the website, you will type in these special codes to view the fun videos. I'm already smiling thinking about you watching our videos. ☺

   IMPORTANT! Always ask your parents before you get on the Internet. There's a lot of junk on the Internet and you need to stay far away from all of it. It's important to protect your eyes and ears from what could harm your heart. So MAKE SURE you get permission! Okay? *Seriously!*

4. During your **HCWG** (short for **Hot Chocolate with God**) adventure, you will read Sweet Truths. These are awesome, incredible words from God's book—the Bible. If you have never read or even opened a Bible, that's totally okay. Just as I have hopefully started a relationship with you through sharing my heart, God (yes, the One who created you and loves you like crazy) wants to share His heart with you too. Incredible—yeah, I know! God shows us His heart through His Word. It's amazing! You'll see.

5. Lastly, you are a treasure! Wrapped up in skin (weird, right?). You were created by God to be exactly you. As you grow and learn more about you and the God who loves you, go! Go and SHARE YOU! Go and SHARE GOD! Wherever you are, go and share the wonders of all that you are! God is with you. ☺

1

Just Me . . . and This Incredible Story Called My Life!

Your life is a story.

It's a journey that God has already mapped out. (Of course, my first thought about this is "If God knows everything about my life, why doesn't He just tell me . . . so I know?") It doesn't work that way, does it? God wrote a life story about you. He wrote one about me. But He doesn't tell us everything. Why not? Well, I guess because He wants us to get to know Him first. He wants us to know who He is—His story. And He wants us to know who He created us to be. This might sound complicated but it's really not.

Your life is an incredible story that God created!

Every single day your story is being told, kinda like a page that gets turned at the end of the day.

No one else can tell your story like you can. This is epic cool! (Yes, "epic" is my new word lately. I think I heard it first out of Justin Bieber's mouth. I just might have to get some super tween girl swag on too. Ha-ha . . . whatever. Let's just have fun!) Maybe you're not happy with your life right now and wish that your life were different, that you were different. **STOP** right now and read the next sentence slowly and carefully! You are beautifully and wonderfully made. **NOTHING** about you is a mistake, because **GOD** *never* makes mistakes! Let this little, I mean **HUGE**, fact sink in.

You are exactly YOU! And who you are is great!

You have a story to tell!

I know, I know—stop talking, Cam, and let's have some fun! I hear you loud and clear.

Well, I'll tell you what, a traveling story can be a whole lot of fun—why don't we sort of warm up with that? Here's how it works: You write the first page or two of a story (be sure others can read it—ha-ha) and then pass it on to a friend. She writes the next page or two and gives it to another friend. After that it gets passed on to as many friends as you decide to include to create a great story. When it's gone round and round a few times, get together, make some hot chocolate (unless it's summer, then make a cold drink), and take turns reading the story. What a blast to see everyone's imagination all ramped up!

So, are you warmed up and ready to get into this or what?

Let's get rolling with seventy-five questions. (SWEET!)

Its time to start sharing, my friend! It's time to have fun being you! Most of these questions are easy, but if you get stuck and find that you don't have an answer, just move on. Don't even worry about it. Oh, and one more thing—this is a safe place. Don't try to be someone you're not. That would be like me trying to be a Transformer or something. You get the point.

Just be YOU!

Seventy-Five Cool, Very Fun Questions About You and Your Awesome Story

1. What's the date today? (Every day, every moment is part of your STORY—and today is especially cool, because you're hangin' out with me!)

2. Where are you right now? Are you at home, in your bedroom? Who's home with you? Did you just leave the bookstore after purchasing this book? Describe where you are and what's happening around you.

3. What are your first, middle, and last names, and nickname?

4. Please print and write (in cursive) your full name.

5. Tricky—now write (or print, if you think it will be easier for you) your name with the opposite hand. If you're right handed, write your name with your left hand.

Now go and have your mom, dad, and siblings write your full name in the space below. Whose handwriting do you like the most? Circle your favorite.

Cam Jam: My full name is Camryn Lynn Kelly. I like my name but here's the deal: I can never find anything cool with my name on it, like fun notepads and pens or whatever. I'm serious. Whenever I find stuff like that, they only make things with my name spelled like this: Cameron—and that's usually the boys' way of spelling. UGH! Oh well! My grandma (my mom's mom) wanted to name me Jacquelyn Rose Kelly. Her name is Jacque Lynn. And from what I was told, she wanted my middle name to be Rose like the girl in the movie *Titanic*. So weird . . . Anyway, my dad won the naming of the baby battle. But my grandma still got Lynn in there.

6. Ask your parents why they decided to name you the way they did. Write down what they tell you.

JUST COOL: I've never done this before but I thought it would be fun. Take the three initials that represent your full name. Mine would be CLK. Now reverse the order and create a new name for yourself. Here's my example: Kaitlin Lorraine Crumpet. Ba-ha-ha-ha! Do you like my new name?

7. Another name game! Write down your full name and then write down all the words that you can make out of your full name. (For instance, from Camryn Lynn Kelly I can create these words: real, learn, elk, army. Do you get it?)

8. Did your parents find out that you were going to be a girl before you were born?

Cam Jam: My parents found out about me, my brother, and my sister, Erin, but that's another story for another time. Can you believe that we have medical technology that can actually determine whether or not a baby will be a boy or a girl? Crazy, right?

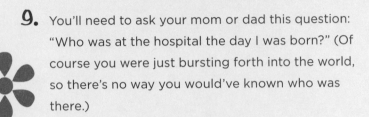

9. You'll need to ask your mom or dad this question: "Who was at the hospital the day I was born?" (Of course you were just bursting forth into the world, so there's no way you would've known who was there.)

10. When is your birthday and how old are you right now?

11. If you could be a different age, how old would you be and why?

12. If you could change your birthday to a different day or time of year—when would you change it to and why?

13. Since we're talking about birthdays, what's your favorite part of a birthday cake? Maybe you like ice cream the best. (I'm a frosting freak!)

14. Have you ever had a surprise birthday party? Were you surprised?

15. What's the best birthday gift you have ever given someone? You know, the kind you wish you could keep for yourself.

16. The best birthday gift you ever received was . . . ?

Cam Jam: Hey—I have something to tell you. You're the gift! Yes, it's true! When you celebrate your birthday I want to remind you that YOU are the gift. God created you to be a blessing to the people in your life. I don't know who wrote or said this but I read it somewhere before, **"Life is God's gift to you. What you do with your life is your gift to God."** I really like this. I hope my life is a gift to others and especially to God. I hope yours is too! Oh, and by the way, my birthday is June 24. I'm a summer birthday girl. Because of this, I usually have to celebrate at the end of the school year with all the other summer kids. But that's okay. Right now, as I write this, I'm twelve years old. I just thought of this—why don't you go and find a current picture of yourself and tape or paste it inside the present frame? I wish I could see you—like really see you, face-to-face. Maybe someday! Remember—YOU are the gift!

YOU Are the Gift!

17. Describe what you look like. Pretend your phone just rang and it's me on the other end and I ask you this question: "What do you look like? Tell me about the girl that you see when you look in the mirror." You know, stuff like eye and hair color, how tall you are, and so on.

18. Okay, I admit it—this is just a random, goofy question. If you could color your hair any color of the rainbow, what color would you choose? Did you pick your favorite color? (I'd choose purple because it's my favorite color right now.)

19. Hey, since we're talking about hair, do either of your parents have gray hair yet? What's up with this, anyway? I don't ever want to have gray hair, do you? Maybe it's a sign of wisdom or something. That's what my mom says. Hmm, I'm not so sure about that. Why does she always try to pull her gray hair out if it brings her wisdom? I'd rather have purple hair. I think.

20. Do you know how to braid? (I've been taught how to braid but I still don't know how to do it on my own hair. I'm sure I'll learn sooner or later.)

JUST COOL: Okay, do you see all that space below? I want you to outline your hand—the one you're holding the pen or pencil with while you're still holding it! NO—hee-hee! The one you're not writing with, of course! Outline it in that space. Then write down (in each finger space) FIVE THINGS about your outer appearance that you are thankful for.

21. What's your address?

22. Who do you live with? (Write down everyone's names and ages right now and don't forget your pets.)

Name	Age

23. Do you still live in the state where you were born? Write down the name of the state you were born in.

24. If you could pick any place in the entire world, where would you want to live?

25. Do you live where you get to experience all four seasons of the year?

26. Where is the farthest place away from home that you have visited? Why were you there?

27. Have you ever been on an airplane? (I don't really like airplanes.)

28. Where did you go the last time you were on an airplane?

Cam Jam: Every year, my family and I fly to Hilton Head Island in South Carolina. We go there as a family to celebrate the life of my brother, Hunter. He went to heaven on August 5, 2005. I miss him every single day. There are so many things I'd like to tell you about Hilton Head but I think I'll show you instead. For even more fun, I'll have my cousins Paige and Ben join us.

CAM CLIPS CODE: HILTON HEAD

29. Warmest state you've ever been to? How hot was it?

30. Coldest state you've ever been to? How cold was it?

31. Yippee, no school! You're snowed in. What are you going to do today?

32. Do you know how to ski or snowboard?

33. Have you ever been on a snowmobile? (Did you fall off? Ba-ha-ha-ha . . .)

34. Have you ever gone snow tubing? (This is so much fun!)

35. Did you ever make a snow angel or build a snowman? What did you use to make his face and dress him up?

Cam Jam: Hey, sorry about all the snow talk. I love snow but I can't stand being cold. Brrr! I live in the great state of New York. When most people hear that you are from New York, they think you live in the city, like New York City. I don't live anywhere near the city. And I'm glad because I'm more of a country girl, except for the bugs and spiders and stuff like that. I get to experience all four seasons: summer, fall, winter, and spring. We are known for snow where I live. We love the snow. I especially like it when we have too much snow and all the schools have to close. Maybe you don't get to see snow where you live. Well, I would like to show you what winter and snow fun looks like for the Kelly family. Come on, check it out!

CAM CLIPS CODE: SNOW FUN

You must read this amazing **Sweet Truth**. I thought I would share this one just in case you have ever wondered who is in charge of our weather here on Earth. The really great thing about this Bible verse is that if God tells the snow and rain what to do, you can be sure that His instructions for you are perfect and good too. He really does know what He's doing.

God's voice thunders in marvelous ways; he does great things beyond our understanding. He says to the snow, "Fall on the earth," and to the rain shower, "Be a mighty downpour." So that everyone he has made may know his work, he stops all people from their labor. —Job 37:5-7

36. Maybe you live where the sun always shines. (Where in the world is this place? I want to visit!) What do you do for fun where you live? For instance, if you live near the ocean, do you go to the beach a lot? Do you surf? (I'm laughing so hard right now just imagining myself getting on a surfboard. Yeah, no way.) If you live near a mountain, do you go hiking and camping in the woods? Have you ever had a picnic with a bear?

37. Speaking of camping, have you ever roasted marshmallows and made s'mores?

38. Have you ever stared too long at the fire and it made your eyes hurt? (I have. Yeah, lesson for campfires— DO NOT stare at the fire.)

39. Did you ever sleep outside in a tent under the beautiful moonlight? If you did, who did you camp with? Did you get a bunch of mosquito bites? (Ouch, they hurt and itch like crazy.)

40. We're talking about sleeping, so I must ask: How many pillows and blankets do you sleep with? Do you have a certain bedtime setup? If you do, describe what it is.

41. Do you sleep with a stuffed animal? If you do, what kind of animal is he (or she) and what's his (or her) name? How long have you been sleeping with it?

Cam Jam: I've never slept in a tent and I think it's safe to say that I never will. Eww! I like the country but give me a bed to sleep in! The closest I get to outdoor living is our family lodge: Hunter's Haven Lodge. My daddy loves to hunt, which is why he named my older brother Hunter. The lodge is named after him. I don't like the fact that my daddy hunts animals, especially since they're so beautiful. But it's something he really, really likes to do, almost as much as he likes football. I'd like to take you to visit Hunter's Haven Lodge. I must warn you in advance, though, that our lodge has a lot of stuffed, dead animals everywhere. I'm sorry if this offends you. My cousin Ben had a hard time getting used to it too. So come along—I have so much to show you. Maybe if we get a chance I'll take you snow tubing with me. Hysterical!

CAM CLIPS CODE: HUNTER'S HAVEN LODGE

42. Can you touch your tongue to your nose? (Odd, I know, but I was just wondering. ☺)

43. Have you won any trophies? For what?

44. Did you ever win a prize, a contest, or a raffle? What did you win?

45. Hey, did you ever win a goldfish at a fair? What did you name him or her?

46. If your family members were animals, what would they be? Yikes! What animal would you be? (I think I would want to be a tiger. And my mommy would be a giraffe—ha-ha! I don't really think she would like to be a giraffe. It's kind of a compliment because my mom has a nice long neck—LOL—but clearly not as long as a beautiful giraffe. Good thing, huh?)

47. Do you like to wear slippers?

48. What do your favorite slippers look like? Do you wear them on your hands or feet?

49. Do you like to go barefoot? (Only at the beach for me.)

50. Do you own a pair of cowboy boots? And while we're thinking cowboy, have you ever gone horseback riding?

Favorites: It seems like my favorites change as I get older. For instance, my favorite muffin used to be chocolate chip, but now it's blueberry. Orange used to be my favorite color, but now it's purple.

51. Favorite time of the day? Why?

52. Favorite day of the week? Why?

53. Favorite meal—breakfast, lunch, or dinner? And what do you like to eat for this meal?

54. This isn't a favorite question but did you ever have a breakfast dinner? (I call this "dinfast" or "breakinner"—goofy, I know. By the way, anybody know what "supper" is? It's not dinner, right? Or are they the same thing? Sheesh . . . let's just eat already!)

Cam Jam: The night before Christmas we always have a breakfast dinner. It's so delicious. Usually my daddy cooks because my mom is busy wrapping gifts or whatever. He cooks typical breakfast stuff like pancakes, eggs, toast, and bacon. Yummy. Just thinking about it makes me hungry. We also have breakfast for dinner on some Sunday evenings. It's usually just cereal. Sunday cereal! We all love cereal in our family. Unfortunately, my parents only let us get sugar cereals every once in a while. Oh well. My very favorite cereal is Lucky Charms. Do you know why? Because they're magically delicious.

Erin: So, Cam, I'm surprised you didn't give away Daddy's little cereal secret. Since you didn't mention it, I thought I should. It's crazy but the truth is, my dad loves Fruity Pebbles cereal. Yeah, certainly not the breakfast of champions. My mom sends him to the grocery store every once in a while and he's always sneaking that sugar cereal into our house. Of course Cam loves it—right, Cam?

55. Favorite cereal?

56. Favorite smell? (Hmm, maybe your socks. SO DISGUSTING! I wonder about something—why do dogs like to chew on smelly, dirty socks? If you know the answer, please fill me in.)

57. Favorite word? (Yeah, I've never thought about this either. I think mine would be Lord or gum.)

58. Favorite kind of muffin?

59. Favorite kind of bagel?

60. Favorite kind of donut?

Cam Jam: My daddy buys donuts and sneaks them into our house all the time—like he does with the cereal. And then he hides them so we can't find them. ARE YOU SERIOUS? I can smell a donut a mile away.

61. Favorite sandwich?

62. Favorite milkshake flavor?

63. Favorite Popsicle flavor?

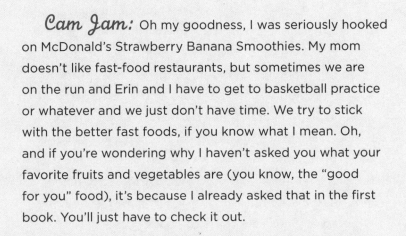

64. Favorite kind of smoothie?

Cam Jam: Oh my goodness, I was seriously hooked on McDonald's Strawberry Banana Smoothies. My mom doesn't like fast-food restaurants, but sometimes we are on the run and Erin and I have to get to basketball practice or whatever and we just don't have time. We try to stick with the better fast foods, if you know what I mean. Oh, and if you're wondering why I haven't asked you what your favorite fruits and vegetables are (you know, the "good for you" food), it's because I already asked that in the first book. You'll just have to check it out.

65. Before we go any further with your favorite things I have to ask you this. Do you think it's important to exercise and eat healthy foods? Why?

66. What types of food do you consider healthy?

67. What's your favorite kind of exercise and how often do you do it (once a week or what)?

Cam Jam: Yes, sorry about the "healthy food" interruption but I'm always learning how important it is to eat right and exercise. My sister Erin works out a lot. She's very athletic and loves to play basketball. During the summer, I get a lot of exercise by swimming almost every day. We're trying to eat better foods too. It's hard to change your eating habits, but it's very important.

We need to take care of our bodies. In fact, God has a lot to say about this very thing. He cares about what we put into our bodies and our minds. In everything we do, we should glorify Him. That word "glory" is something I don't fully understand. So I decided to look it up in the dictionary. I think it's pretty awesome that Jesus Christ is actually mentioned under "glory" in this dictionary version. He should be! Please read the **Sweet Truth** and definition of "glory." We have so much to learn, don't we? Maybe that's why God gives us an entire life to do it.

Sweet Truth

So whether you eat or drink or whatever you do, do it all for the glory of God.
—1 Corinthians 10:31

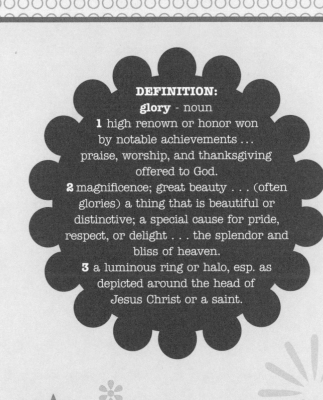

DEFINITION:
glory - noun
1 high renown or honor won by notable achievements . . . praise, worship, and thanksgiving offered to God.
2 magnificence; great beauty . . . (often glories) a thing that is beautiful or distinctive; a special cause for pride, respect, or delight . . . the splendor and bliss of heaven.
3 a luminous ring or halo, esp. as depicted around the head of Jesus Christ or a saint.

I think now is a good time to stop for a quick prayer. Doing all things to the glory of God isn't easy. So let's ask God for some help with this. I'll get us started, and you can finish it up. Deal?

Dear God,

You love us and care about the details of our lives. We need Your help to live a life that pleases You in every way. Please help us to know and love You more so we can live a life that honors You . . .

68. All this talk about food is making me hungry, so I just have to ask . . . are you snacking on something right now? What?

What was the last thing you ate?

69. If you could eat your favorite snack right now, what would you be eating?

70. Favorite soda pop?

71. Favorite lollipop (or sucker, whatever you call it)?

72. Favorite gum?

73. Favorite candy bar?

Cam Jam: I'm cracking up right now. Can you tell that I have a sweet tooth? If you haven't figured it out already with all the sweet stuff going on in this book: **Sweet Truths, Sweet Sections**, and the last few favorite questions. Yeah, I admit it. I love candy. When I was a little kid I used to hide candy and gum all over the house in random places. Under the living room couch pillows. In my bedroom closet. In little baggies stuffed in my sock and underwear drawers. (Now that I'm thinking about it, it's kind of gross that I hid candy in my sock and underwear drawers. Hmm.) I thought for sure my mom would never catch on to my candy hide and seek. But she did. She cares too much about me to let me eat candy all day. Because I used to get a little out of control with my sugar cravings I now have to ask my parents before I can eat candy. Sometimes I forget to ask, but most of the time I remember. It's just that it tastes so good. Can you relate? Do you know what I mean?

Erin: Cam, I think you used to hide candy in my room too. In fact, I'm pretty sure I found some of last year's Halloween candy tucked behind some books in my bookcase. Was that you? Just curious.

74. So what's your favorite pen? *I'm serious!*

Cam Jam: I'm a huge pen fan! Yes, I think I've tried every single pen ever made. Well, maybe. When you journal like I do, you need a good writing pen. It doesn't matter what store I'm in, you'll find me searching for yet another smooth, colorful pen. My mommy and sister feel the same way I do. In fact, we decided to test all of our pens to determine which ones are the very best. We narrowed it down to the top five. To find out what these are, you can go to the website and click on **Girl Talk** and then click on **Girl Stuff**. Here you'll find **The Top Five Pens in the World**. By the way, this is just our opinion. You might know of a very cool pen that we haven't listed. Please send us a message through the website and tell us what kind of pen is your favorite. ☺ Happy pen shopping!

Hold on! Let's do something different. I love this part! I'm sure you've heard of the game "Would You Rather."

 Well, that's what this is. Circle one of the choices in the two columns on the next page that you would choose if you had to. Yes, these are just random questions, but it's fun—and you know it!

 I've shared some of what I would rather do in parentheses. (Just in case you don't know what I mean, the first choice—would you rather have a hamster or a hedgehog for a pet?)

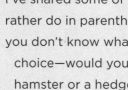

Would You Rather...

Have a hamster (*We had a hamster. His name was Winslow and he smelled really bad.*)	Have a hedgehog
Eat noodles plain (*butter and salt, please*)	Eat noodles with sauce
Eat french fries	Eat onion rings
Go dancing (*all the time*)	Hunt for worms
Cook a meal	Let Mommy cook
Soak up the sun in Alaska	Downhill ski without snow
Play hide and seek	Play tag
Eat fresh fruit (*gotta love raspberries*)	Eat fresh veggies (*carrots only!*)
Eat candy	Eat rocks with sugar

Okay, time to finish up the rest of the **Seventy-Five Cool, Very Fun Questions . . . About You and Your Awesome Story**. **Finish well, my friend!**

75. And finally—drum roll, please . . . Just curious, how do you feel about fruit flies? (Our house got attacked by them once and it was so GROSS!)

And you thought I was going to end this section with an intense question. Ha! Sorry about that. There's so much more to this book than you thought, right? Let's keep going. Unless, of course, you need to go to the bathroom or your mom just said, "It's time for dinner." Or "Go to bed."

Stick with me!

Oops, I almost forgot. (Ugh, how could I forget?) The word search! Let's find things related to **Hot Chocolate with God**. Have fun! See you in Sweet Section 2!

Time yourself (or have someone else time you) to see how long it takes you to complete this word search. Jot down your time right here _____

.

Are you ready? GO!

Hot Chocolate with God

```
H F L V K I M L V Y F O I F C
J O A U X A A O A W V P R B I
W P T I A Y F V Z L M I W I G
X E S C T E M E D U E L E G W
M G F I H H A A B N I A S X G
O A R L L O C O D F E I W Q O
U U J S U G C S E H S Z E P Q
P Q J M G S H O R T S U E M Q
P S A F A I J D L Z X X T Z B
N U F V P C W I U A U U T G I
G I R L S M U F X U T I R O Z
I K G G Q S Z H Z J H E U B Z
P C E D Z R P T Q J S C T X C
S P I L C M A C K S B S H Q F
M W Y Z A Z T M K N C M S G O
```

CAM CLIPS	CAM FAM	CAM JAM
FAITH	FRIENDSHIP	FUN
GIRLS	HOT CHOCOLATE	LIFE
LOVE	PURITY	SWEET TRUTHS

Sweet Section

2

My Fears, Faith, and the Real Me

It's true, there's more to you than what you see when you look in the mirror. You're not just skin and a bunch of bones, with hair in all sorts of places and teeth and—well, you know what I mean. You're more than what people see on the outside. Someone might look into your eyes, hold your hand, and even whisper in your ear, but your eyes, hands, and ears *aren't you* . . .

The real YOU is what's on the inside!

Your heart!

Your soul!

What makes you YOU, that's what this section is all about.

We'll talk about some things in this section that you probably don't want to talk about, like what you're afraid of and stuff like that. But remember, this is your book. If there's something I've asked you that you don't feel like answering, that's okay. I understand. Just move on to the next question or section. I want you to have fun here. I also hope you feel like you can pour out all that's on the inside here too.

I share my heart (my inside) best through journaling.

Sometimes I find it hard to express myself, so I write down how I'm feeling in my journals. You should try it.

I know I've already said this before, in the first book and in this one, but I must say it again.

You are the only *you* God has ever, and will ever, create! No one can be YOU—but YOU!

There will never, ever be another *you*. No one can take your place! Wow! This is incredible!

So . . . as we laugh, cry, and hopefully pray together, just be yourself . . . the one God loves like crazy.

To get the ball rolling, let's start off with . . .

Ten Reasonable, Random Questions

1. Did you ever get gum stuck in your hair so bad that you had to have it cut out?

2. What do you wish you could do, but can't? (Hmm, I have a long list for this, starting with a candy store in my house.)

3. Did you ever have a dream about a unicorn or flying monkeys or any other unusual animals?

4. What's your favorite day of the year?

5. If you had a pet chipmunk, what would you name him/her? (I think A.J. is a great name.)

6. If you could change one thing about yourself, what would it be?

7. What card games do you know how to play?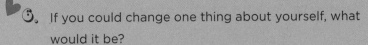

8. Do you like worms—I mean gummy worms?

9. Have you ever been in a food fight?

10. What snack do you always have while driving around in the car? (BBQ chips are a must.)

Just Me ... Being Me

Use these two pages to be YOU. Cut words or pictures out of magazines or whatever that tell the story of you. Be CREATIVE! Use photos. Draw. Whatever. It's your own personal graffiti wall! If someone were to open to these two pages, they should get a good idea of what you're all about.

(I would have a picture of the Bible, my family, candy wrappers, the word "dance," a picture of a basketball, stuff like that.)

Here's another very hip, creative thing for you to do. (Hmm . . . time-out here! What's "hip" have to do with anything? No one says that anymore. Easy there, Cam, going a little retro there?) Anyhow, so how about this— design your own logo, a logo that would represent who you are. When people see it, they would say, "Oh, [your name] made this." (For me they would say, "Oh, Cam Kelly made this.") For example, when you see the Nike swoosh thing, you know what it is, right? So design a logo that's YOU.)

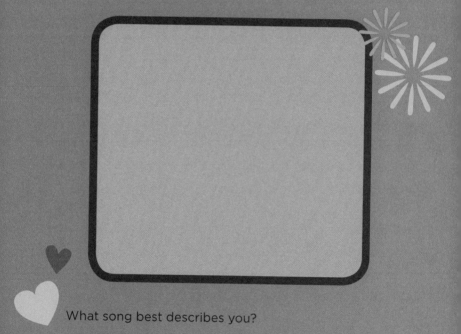

What song best describes you?

Write down the lines from that song that really describe you.

What's your favorite song right now?

By the way, what kind of music do your parents listen to?

Cam Jam: My dad is a country music freak. He also likes what he calls "classic rock," I have no idea what that is. Hmm, maybe that's because he's a classic! I guess it's his kind of music from the seventies, when he grew up—which seems so long ago. Wow! My daddy can't stand rap music or any hip-hop stuff. Yeah, probably because he doesn't really know how to dance. Ha-ha—you should see him try. Oh boy! When he drives, my sissy and I have to listen to his music. It's okay when it's country because we've learned to like it. Sometimes he starts dancing while he's driving. Not a pretty sight. I just want to say to him, "Keep your hands on the wheel, Daddy!" He's so funny. My mom, on the other hand, loves Christian music. Erin and I have only been allowed to listen to "secular" music for, like, a year. Secular music is all other music except Christian. Some of it is good but some of it is really bad, like with bleeped-out words and stuff. My mom controls the radio, so we're safe.

Who controls the radio in your car?

Who has a better singing voice, your mom or dad or maybe one of your siblings? Do you have a good voice?

Is there a certain song that you just cannot listen to? (If this song comes on, you must change the station.)

Cam Jam: There are a few songs that I absolutely cannot listen to. Ever since my brother, Hunter, went to heaven when I was only six years old, there are certain songs that remind me of him. It's not that I don't want to think about Hunter. I think about him all the time. It's just that music isn't only what you hear, it's what you feel when you hear it, and these songs always make me cry. Crying is good, but not when I'm on my way to school—if you know what I mean.

What movie have you watched at least a hundred times?

Why do you like this movie?

What is the WORST movie you ever saw?

What made it so bad?

What movies made you laugh your head off? (By the way, I'm so thankful that we can't actually laugh our heads right off—yikes.)

Since we're talking about LAUGHING . . . what's the funniest video you've watched on the Internet?

Funniest person you know?

Funniest thing one of your family members has ever done?

Top two things you think about most of the time:

1.

2.

Top two things you'd rather not think about:

1.

2.

(Oops, sorry for making you think about those two things.)

Can you think of something you've NEVER thought about before? (Hmm.)

Are you creative?

Do you have a special craft or talent that you can do, like knitting or drawing or getting a black belt in karate? What is it and what have you made?

Cam Jam: I guess you could say that I'm sort of crafty and talented. I'm pretty good at making flower pens and bookmarks. You can check this out at **www.hotchocolatewithgod.com**. My grandma is amazing at crafts. She's so talented, especially on the sewing machine. I think I need to show you just how crafty she is. Let's go to her house and watch her make something fun for **Hot Chocolate with God**. How about a pen and pencil case or a cool carry bag or something? This will be great, especially if you've never met Grammie before. She's an incredible woman. You'll see. Let's go!

CAM CLIPS CODE: CRAFTY GRAMMIE

Are you full of energy and surprises all the time? Do your friends and family wonder what you'll think of and do next?

Do you love a challenge or are you happier when things go smoothly all the time?

Cam Jam: Um, yeah—things don't always go smoothly. Just sayin' . . .

Do you have a grateful heart and attitude?

Do your parents still have to remind you to say "please" and "thank you"?

Cam Jam: Fine, I admit I'm human. It's true. Sometimes I still forget to say "please" and "thank you." This is not something I'm proud of. In fact, I feel bad when I forget, especially when my parents have to remind me in front of others. Not cool. You know what? I'm going to pray about this right now. God's the only one who can help me remember. He knows my heart. I'll be right back.

Do you try to always listen and do what you're told?

Do you help out around the house without being asked?

OUT OF THE BLUE
Thoughts and Questions

Where is the "BLUE" that this stuff comes out of anyway? And what's with the "BLUE"? I mean, why not OUT OF THE RED, or GRAY, or even OUT OF THE STRIPES, or DOTS, or OUT OF THE JELL-O PUDDING? Hey, how about OUT OF THE HOT CHOCOLATE? Ha-ha! Just sayin'. Okay?

Do you own a poncho—the kind from Mexico? (Ba-ha-ha-ha—so random. I know, very goofy.)

Hey, speaking of random, what's the most random thing you've ever done? That you've seen anyone else do?

What are your thoughts regarding black nail polish?

Do you bite your toenails? (Um, gross, but I think we've all been there, done that when we were little babies. Can you picture it—the "foot in the mouth" photo that all parents love to take of their babies. Super gross! But as infants we really don't know any better, do we?)

Have you ever painted your face for a homecoming football game or something like that?
What did you look like?

When you get to have your face painted, what do you usually ask the person to paint on your face? (I've been a tiger and butterfly before.)

Do you think Zelfie and Maple are cute puppy names?

What other dog or cat names do you like?

Did you ever wish you could smash a plate against the wall or on the ground? (I wish I could. Does this mean I have anger issues?)

Has anyone ever given you flowers?
Who?   What was the occasion?

Why do you think God put thorns on roses? That really bugs me!

What's the coolest thing that happened to you in the last year? Write down everything you remember.

Do you remember anything that happened to you in 1741? (Oh wait, we weren't even alive back then, never mind.)

Where do you hide something when you don't want anyone to find it? (Psst, I won't tell. ☺ I usually hide things in my closet.)

Go look under your bed right now and write down what you find. (Yes, dust bunnies count.)

If you could be invisible for a day, what would you do?

What if you could be a Transformer, what would you change into? A car? Frog? Trampoline? Peanut butter sandwich?

What new words have you learned lately?

Have you ever gone rock climbing before? For real or on a rock wall?

Do you turn all red and blotchy when you get embarrassed or when you cry? (I get all blotchy when I cry and so does my mom.)

Okay, okay—back to the more serious questions.

What are you most afraid of right now? (Spiders—eww.)

Cam Jam: Yes, I'm afraid of spiders and bees. Hate them! But since I've asked you to be real with me, I should be open about this with you as well. I'm afraid of something happening to my parents. I don't like when they go out of town on an airplane. What if their plane crashes? I'm not supposed to worry, but it's hard not to sometimes. My mother tells me to pray about my fears because God doesn't want me to worry or be afraid. When I pray, I do feel better. It's really about trusting God with everything. I hope that as I grow I can trust Him more and more every single day.

What do you usually do when you're afraid?

Write down three things that break your heart and explain why they hurt you. 💜

1.

2.

3.

What made you cry recently? Why?

Tell me how you are feeling right this very minute. Is anything bothering you? Are you mad at someone? Worried? Afraid? Excited about something? Is everything in your life going super great right now? *Talk to me.* Use the journal paper to tell me all about it. I already got you started. Hee-hee . . .

Dear Camryn

Cam Jam: It's okay to express your feelings. Keeping everything bottled up inside isn't healthy. God created us with emotions and the ability to express them. I don't know what I would do if I couldn't cry—or laugh. How you feel is very important to God. He has feelings too and understands ours, so He wants you to talk to Him about anything and everything as often as you want to. It's called a relationship. God isn't up there in heaven too busy for you. He's not up there waiting for you to make a mistake so

He can yell at you—NO WAY! He isn't worried about what's going to happen to you. No, He loves you and is with you all the time. You are NEVER alone. Never! He created you and knows exactly what you need at all times. Isn't this a huge relief? Nothing surprises God! So talk to Him. Get to know Him. Tell Him about your day, just like you shared with me.

Erin: Okay, I admit it, I tend to keep things bottled up inside most of the time. My mom says I'm a lot like Daddy. I don't like to talk about what's going on in my heart and mind. Of course I pray and tell God everything, but I don't talk to others that often. Mom tells me that God has placed people in my life to encourage and guide me. I'm starting to open up and share more, but I'm still not comfortable talking about my deepest feelings. Maybe this will change for me. But even if it doesn't, I know God is always with me. He is listening and He understands me better than anyone.

Sweet Truth

Don't worry about anything; instead, pray about everything. Tell God what you need, and thank him for all he has done. If you do this, you will experience God's peace, which is far more wonderful than the human mind can understand. His peace will guard your hearts and minds as you live in Christ Jesus. — Philippians 4:67 (NLT)

Now, let's talk about your faith. First of all, what is faith exactly? If you look it up in the dictionary, the following is what you'll find.

And . . . if you look it up in God's Word, the Bible—well, THAT'S a **Sweet Truth**, read it for yourself:

DEFINITION:
faith - noun
1 complete trust or confidence in someone or something.
2 strong belief in God or in the doctrines of a religion . . .
• a system of religious belief.
• a strongly held belief or theory.

Faith is being sure of what you hope for and certain of what you do not see. —Hebrews 11:1

What do you think this **Sweet Truth** means?

Do you think God knows and cares about every detail that's going on in your life?

Do you believe that your future is in God's hands?
If you answered yes, how do you know? If you answered no,
why?

Are you honest with God?

Complete the sentences below:

Sometimes I wonder . . .

I wish my parents . . .

I wish my friends . . .

I wish God . . .

I like to be alone when . . .

It's hard to trust God when . . .

I worry most about . . .

I believe that . . .

The Real Me Crisscross Puzzle

5. Don't try to be someone you're not. Always be _____.
7. Complete trust in God.
8. It's better to _____ God than be afraid.
9. Cam's favorite color.
10. A place to write down your thoughts and feelings.
12. GOD IS ALWAYS with you. You are never _____!
13. Don't worry. Pray about _____.
14. Another word for talking to God.

1. Cam's mom likes _____ music.
2. You were created for a _____.
3. What you should be drinking while you do this puzzle.
4. Man looks at the outward appearance, but God looks at your _____.
6. The real you is what's on the _____.
9. God's _____ will guard your heart and mind.
11. Cam's dad likes _____ music.

Friendship . . . Ups and Downs and the In-Between Stuff

When I think about friendship and what my friends mean to me, the first thing that comes to my mind is this verse: "A friend loves at all times" (Proverbs 17:17).

When God says all, He means all—meaning every, not leaving anything out. So I have to ask myself, "Camryn, do you love your friends at all times?" Hmm.

Do you?

To be honest with you, I think it's hard to love my friends all the time. But the good thing is, God is always helping me to be more loving every day. I need His love in me in order to love others the way I should, the way I really want to, the way God wants me to.

We all go through rough times with our friends. I know I have had some ups and downs with mine. But you know what, we're all going to go through struggles. Sometimes that's how we learn. (At least that's what my mom says.)

It's what you do about it that counts. (My daddy ALWAYS says that.)

Ha—I'm trying to share what my mom and dad teach me, can you tell?

I really want to be a *true and faithful* friend, don't you?

I know I need God's help to be the best friend I can possibly be.

This is so hard sometimes, and my mommy told me that a lot of it has to do with expectations. (Big word, expectations.) Let me explain. When you set your expectations of your friends really high (like you expect them to be a certain way), at some point you will be disappointed. Our friends can't always be who we want them to be, just like we can't always be who our friends want us to be. We are not perfect people.

Remember this, God will never let you down and He will fulfill every expectation.

So let's talk about *tween girl* friendships.

I can't wait to hear what you have to say!

Friends and Best Friends . . . oh, and the "Frenemy"

First of all, I think it's possible to have friends and best friends. I could be wrong about this and please tell me if I am. Here's the deal. I have people that I would consider friends in school. But I wouldn't share my heart and special secrets with them. The important things I only share with my best friends. Does this make sense?

Oh, and the "frenemy" . . . we'll talk about her too and what to do about her. Hmm, yeah.

So, who are your friends? (Write their names below and write down ONE WORD that best describes each of your friends.)

Friends

Cam Jam: Hey, believe it or not, boys can be friends too. It's funny, because my mom even said that sometimes boys can be better friends than girls. I haven't experienced this yet so I don't know. What do you think? Since boys are so different—they burp and toot and do gross things—I can't imagine that they could be the kind of friend that a girl can be. I'll let you know if this changes for me since I am getting older.

Erin: Cam, you know that I have boys that are just friends. I agree that sometimes boys can be better friends than girls, but so far for me, my best friends are still closer than the boys I have as friends. The tricky thing when it comes to boys being friends is that sometimes you start liking the boy that's your friend, or he starts liking you, and then everything just gets really awkward. My teen advice is to have a handful of close friends—and if a few of them are boys, cool—and just stay friends. Yeah, I think I've said enough on this for now.

Do you have any boy friends? (Not *boyfriends*, silly, boys that are just friends.) Write their names below, please. And just like the list above, write down ONE WORD that best describes these boys. (Be nice—don't write "smelly" or anything like that. Okay?)

Boy Friends

Nine Questions about Your Friends

Write down the name of your friend who best fits the answers to these questions.

1. She lives the closest to me —

2. She gets on my nerves the most —

3. I like the way she dresses —

4. She makes me laugh . . . a lot —

5. I would miss her if she moved far away —

6. I'd like to get to know her better —

7. She's the best listener —

8. She gives really good advice —

9. She's so generous —

Who do you think will be your friend forever? (Like, still friends while you're in college and maybe she would even be in your wedding. Or maybe your grandchildren will play together when you babysit them—wow, now THAT'S weird!)

Off-topic QUESTION: If there were no white wedding dresses in the entire world, what COLOR wedding dress would you wear?
And one more thing, what color would you like the girls in your wedding to wear?

Sorry, I just have to ask since I got off topic about the wedding thing. ☺ If you were to get married right now (OH MY GOODNESS—are you KIDDING ME? Of course this won't happen but use your imagination) . . .

Who would you ask to be your maid of honor and bridesmaids?

YIKES—who would you marry? (Oh boy!) And . . . why?

Have you ever been in a wedding? Describe the dress you had to wear and what you did. Flower girl?

I sort of don't want to ask these next questions, but my mom is making me. Ha-ha! Just joking. But really, these are hard ones to answer because you might not want to be honest. Remember, you're safe with me. You're safe here. You're safe with GOD! You can be YOU on these pages. Besides, NO ONE is perfect but GOD. We are all a work in progress. God started the good things He is doing in you and He will finish His work. Which makes me think of two really cool **Sweet Truths**. Check them out before we go any further.

And I am sure that God, who began the good work within you, will continue his work until it is finally finished on that day when Christ Jesus comes back again. — Philippians 1:6 (NLT)

And we know that in all things God works for the good of those who love him, who have been called according to his purpose. —Romans 8:28

Just curious, what do you think these two **Sweet Truths** mean?

I have something very important I want you to do before we go any further. Here's what you'll need in order to complete this task: a piece of paper (this can be any color you want), like half the size of a sheet of lined school paper, a recent picture of yourself, a colorful pen, and some tape.

On the piece of paper, please write the following:

God LOVES me—just the way I am! I'm a work in progress, and God isn't finished with me yet. He has started an awesome work in me and He will complete it. God will work everything in my life together for my good and for His GLORY!

After you write the above, please tape your picture near the words somewhere on the paper. Now . . . tape this **Sweet Truth** reminder somewhere in your house where you will look at it at least once a day. I'm thinking maybe where your clothes are or in the bathroom. Most important, read this and **BELIEVE** it . . . because it's true!

Okay—no more procrastinating (that's a big word). Please answer the following five questions that might make you squirm and scream.

The Squirmy, Screamy Kinds of Questions

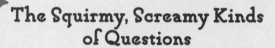

1. Have you ever felt left out by your friends? Share your experience.

2. Are you jealous of any of your friends? (Do you wish you had a nicer house, like your friend does? Do you wish you were prettier, like she is? Hmm . . .) Maybe you're not the jealous one. Do you have a friend who is jealous of you?

3. Have you ever gossiped about one of your friends? (Did one of your friends tell you something and ask you not to tell, but you did? Or maybe you talked bad about a friend just because everyone else was talking about her?) Unfortunately, we've all done this. Let's talk about it.

4. Have you ever just stood by while one of your friends bullied and made fun of a kid in your class? (You knew it was wrong, but you were afraid to say something because you were afraid your friend would start making fun of you.) Write about what happened.

5. Did you ever have a friend for a while and then all of a sudden she decided out of nowhere that she didn't want to be your friend anymore? (She's your friend,

or at least you thought she was, and then for no reason at all she tells you, "I don't want to be your friend anymore." Or stops returning your calls and stuff like that. OUCH—this one hurts. Or maybe you did this to someone? Hmm . . .) Talk about it.

I'm sort of glad we're done with those questions. But it's good to talk about this kind of stuff, especially if you want to be a good friend. I think we all go through the things we just talked about.

Cam Jam: Well, I've experienced all of what you just answered. I've felt left out. In fact, this is something I struggled a lot with in fifth grade. I know now that part of what was happening at the time is that I really only had one BFF. And when she started hanging out with other friends I got jealous (yuck!). The jealousy made me not very fun to be around because I was cranky. But I learned from this. And you will too. Don't ever give up on yourself. God never gives up on you. Yikes, I hate to admit this next one—but I can because I know that God has already forgiven me. And because of that I can be honest and share this with you. I've been in a conversation before and said things that I shouldn't because everyone else was. And I don't know which was worse, saying what I shouldn't or being too afraid of others not to say it! BOTH are SO WRONG! Ugh! I felt so bad and knew that I should've kept my mouth shut. Again, I'm learning. I always need God's help and so do you. Then there's the question about the bully friend. Well, if your friend is a bully, you need to get another friend—like RIGHT NOW. If you stand by and let your friend be a bully, you're just as rotten as she is. WHOA! Did I just say that? Yes, because it's true. Like my daddy always says, "You are who you hang out with." You need to defend the person being made fun of instead of letting your friend hurt her with words. If you don't do anything, it's like you're the bully too. Hey, you're not perfect. It's good to talk about these things so that we can help one another become the best friends we possibly can be.

What's your definition of a BEST FRIEND?

Erin: So we're going to talk about best friends and I was thinking . . . maybe you don't have a best friend. Maybe you have trouble making friends and sort of feel very alone in the friend department. I want you to know something. You are NEVER alone! God is with you. He is the BEST FRIEND you can ever have. So let's talk to Him about this before we go any further. I'll get you started and you share your heart too.

Dear God,
Thank you for the gift of friendship. You are the best friend I could ever have. Please help me to know You as my closest and best friend. Help me to trust that You will never leave me and that all of my deepest secrets, hopes, and dreams are safe with You.

Who is your best friend? (Write her name in the bow on top of the gift box and put a picture of her inside the box)

How long have you known your BFF?

What *one* word would you use to describe her?

Tell me about your best friend's family, like how many brothers and sisters does she have? Where does she live? What is the one thing you like best about her? Write down as much information as you know about her.

ALL ABOUT MY BEST FRIEND

Seven SUPER IMPORTANT Questions to Ask Yourself about Your BEST FRIEND

1. **Is she trustworthy?** (Can you tell her anything and everything and know beyond a shadow of a doubt that she WILL NOT TELL ANYONE?)

2. **Does she encourage me?** (Okay, so when you spend time together does she build you up and make you feel good about who you are? The opposite of this would be if she says things to bring you down.)

3. **Can I count on her?** (If you need her help, is she there for you no matter what? If you're not feeling well, is she one of the first people to ask you if you need anything? You know—like does she make you a handmade card when you're home sick, stuff like that?)

4. **Does she care more about herself than others?** (In other words, is she selfish? Do you always have to do what she wants to do in order for her to have fun? Hmm, yikes! Sometimes I'm like this. I need prayer too. Because I don't want to be selfish at all.)

5. **Do I have fun with her?** (You don't have to have everything in common with your BFF, but it's good to always have fun together. Some people just are not meant to be friends. Do you know what I mean?)

☺. **When something really great happens, is she happy with you and for you?** (This is a good question for sure. If your best friend isn't happy for you when something great happens in your life, she's probably jealous. Jealousy is very nasty and can ruin a friendship.)

7. **Last but truly the most important—does she have a strong FAITH in the LORD?** (Okay, maybe I shouldn't have said a "strong" faith because even a weak faith is a good faith. We're all growing and learning to trust God every single day, right? Anyway, true BFFs really do need to have Jesus in their hearts first before they can be best friends to each other.)

Two OFF THE WALL things about your BFF:

1.

2.

How often do you and your BFF get together during the week outside of school?

If you had to pick ONE THING that you are most thankful for about your BFF, what would that one thing be?

Okay—now go and write a letter and tell her. I'm serious. ☺ Go grab some paper, a card or whatever (use a gum wrapper if you have to, ha-ha-ha, that would be me) and tell her how thankful you are for her, including the one thing you wrote down above. I'll be watching to make sure you do this. Um, yeah. I'm going to do it too for my BFF.

What's one thing about you that even your best friend doesn't know?

Hey, that letter is a great idea, but I was thinking— we should do some fun things to show our BFFs that we appreciate them. Here are some ideas:

1. Send her a card with a handmade gift certificate in it to help her with her chores or whatever. (The Kelly girls are big on sending cards.)

2. How about making a collage of photos of you and her along with a special message made from words and pictures cut out of magazines.

3. Or . . . there's the haunting by the hidden note! Every now and then when you're at her house, come prepared with a few notes of appreciation. Then hide them in various places like her pillowcase, book bag, school books, the pockets of her clothes or jackets, and so on. You get the idea—we all like to feel like we are special, and BFFs are really special!

Now I have something else on my mind. You'll have to get with your BFF so you can ask her the following questions.

Seven Very Important, Must-Know Questions for Your Best Friend

1. Do you snore or talk in your sleep?

2. Have you ever walked into the boys' bathroom by mistake? (I did once, OOPS!)

3. Is there anything that you'd like me to pray about for you?

4. Have you ever gotten lost or separated from your parents? (SCARY.)

5. Do you like to eat raw cookie dough? (YUMMY!)

6. Have you ever tried to pluck your eyebrows or nose hairs? (OUCH!)

7. Do you know how to bait a hook with a worm and fish? Oh, and if you catch a fish do you know how to take it off the hook by yourself?

Cam Jam: Well, I'm laughing right now just thinking about how much fun I've had fishing with friends. I think it would be best to take you with me so you can see for yourself. The only place I've ever been fishing is Two Sisters Pond at Hunter's Haven Lodge. So come along and I'll share this very fun and interesting adventure with you. Beware—my friends Bailey, Kiley, and Ally just might freak you out with their fishing skills. Ba-ha-ha-ha . . .

ᴊCAM CLIPS CODE: FISHING

What would you say is the nicest thing you've ever done for one of your friends?

What's the nicest thing one of your friends has done for you?

Cam Jam: I have to admit you can do a lot of nice things for your friends. You can send a card for no reason. You can write an encouraging letter and secretly put it in her school locker. You can just give your friend a hug if it looks like she's having a hard day. There are so many creative things you can do. However, I think the best thing you can do is PRAY! Yes, pray! We all need prayer. Maybe you don't know how to pray. That's okay. Prayer is just talking to God. Of course, talking to God is a BIG deal that should never be taken lightly. Even so, you should never be afraid to talk to Him about anything, anytime. He wants us to share everything with Him. It's all about the relationship . . . remember.

So let's pray right now. First, let's ask God to help us be a great friend to others. He will help us because He wants our friendships to honor Him and make Him smile. ☺ After that we'll ask God to help our friends to be godly and loving—and whatever else we want to pray about. I'll start this prayer and you finish it, okay?

Dear Heavenly Father,
You created friendship, so we need Your help to be the best kind of friend we possibly can be. The Bible says that a friend loves at all times. Please help us to love our friends all the time—especially when it's hard. Help us to be patient, kind, encouraging, and always ready to forgive . . .

GROSS THINGS that we all must deal with from time to time . . .

Have you ever walked out of a bathroom with toilet paper stuck to the bottom of your shoe? (UGH—embarrassing!)

Or that renegade dryer sheet that falls out of your pant leg at just the wrong time? Sheesh!

Okay, this has to be the worst. Did you ever have toilet paper coming out of your pants? (I'm laughing my head off right now even though this is not funny at all if it happens.)

What about the dreaded zipper down in school? (Just horrible.) Has it happened to you?

Then there's the totally classy burp that slipped out in front of the cutest boy in your class. Did this ever happen to you? It's amazing how many shades of red a girl can turn—OUCH!

What do you do when your friend has something in her nose or food stuck between her teeth? (You'd better tell her—that's what friends are for. Seriously!)

What if your friend has bad breath—like really bad. Do you offer her mints and gum? Or do you tell it like it is?

83

Eww . . . have you ever lost your cookies (barfed) in school or in front of one of your friends? If you did and she's still your friend—she's a keeper for sure.

Did you ever forget the nose check?

Cam Jam: So, we Kelly girls, we do something called the "nose check." What in the world is a nose check? Well, before we get out of the car to go into school or somewhere, my mom says, "Nose check." This is a reminder for Erin and me to grab a mirror and check our noses to make sure we don't have to—well, you know, blow or pick, if you get what I'm saying. Gross—yeah, I know. But wouldn't you rather check to make sure your nose is clean instead of walk around all day with a boogey trying to peek out. Eww!

Erin: Oh my goodness, I can't believe Cam just told you about the nose check. That's like Kelly girl inside information or something. JUST JOKING! Actually, it's an important girl thing, for sure.

Lastly, ugh! I really didn't even want to talk about this but we need to. The FRENEMY. What is it? Or should I say, who is she? I'm sure there are a lot of different definitions for this but let's stick with mine for now—since I'm writing this book (hee-hee).

Here's what I would call a "frenemy"—this is someone who pretends like she's your friend for as long as it's convenient for her. In other words, she acts like she's your friend until someone better comes along. Then, when she decides to ditch you, she acts like you don't even exist. Worse than that, she's mean to you and makes fun of you. Yikes! This really STINKS!

Have you ever had a frenemy?

Talk about your experience with her. What happened?

Are you still mad at her for how she treated you?

Do you sometimes want to be mean right back to her? How do you handle this?

Cam Jam: Well, as unfair and hard as this is, you must always treat people the way you would want them to treat you. God will give you the strength to do this. He will. He knows when you are weak. He knows how you're feeling. And ya know what? God loves your enemies or "frenemies" just as much as He loves you. Check out the **Sweet Truth** to see what we need to know about how to handle these types of people. Whoa—LOVE YOUR ENEMIES! I need help with this, don't you?

Sweet Truth

But I tell you, love your enemies and pray for those who persecute you, that you may be children of your Father in heaven. —Matthew 5:44-45

By the way, or BTW if you're texting, friendship isn't limited to people you're already close with; you can *be a friend* to anyone. For example, summer is pretty hot around here, so how about meeting the mailman, newspaper-delivery person, or even a next-door neighbor who's out working in the yard with a cold glass of water, juice, or lemonade, and maybe a plate of brownies? Don't wait to be the difference, go for it. Be a friend to make a friend!

Sweet Truth

A friend loves at all times. —Proverbs 17:17

Let's end this chapter with a **Cam Clip**. Since my sissy, Erin, is a teenager, let's see what she has to say about friendships. Let's ask her some of the questions you just answered. She really is a godly girl and although she won't let me use her mascara and wear her shoes sometimes, she's still a great example for me.

 CAM CLIPS CODE: ERIN TALKS FRIENDSHIPS

Sweet Section

4

Family . . . All About Those Special People You Live With

●♥●♥●♥●♥●♥●♥●♥●♥●♥●♥●♥●♥●♥●♥●

Family.

You live with them.

You eat with them.

You eat them. (No! Ha-ha. At least you'd better not.)

You celebrate birthdays and holidays with them.

You cry with them when life isn't going very well and cheer with them when everything is great.

You even kick back and watch TV with them!

Cam Jam: Speaking of TV, did you know that you can have too much of a good thing? Like, did you ever pile on the candy till you got a stomachache? Well, too much TV kind of gets you "zombiefied," so every now and then I suggest Cam's prescription for TV-head: TV-Turn-Off Week. Instead of TV, try one of these sweet suggestions to fill your sweet time . . .

1. Flash back to your younger years (in a good way) and break out the Play-Doh! Did you know you can actually make your own? Hmm, I just might have to do a **Cam Clip** about this.

2. Have a family talent show. Maybe I could get my daddy to dance, although I've caught him bustin' a move and all I can say is: "YIKES!"

3. Finally . . . make homemade hot chocolate and read **Hot Chocolate with God**! Of course, what else did you expect? HCWG rulz! (That's because God rules.)

Family can mean a lot of different things, depending on the type of family you have. Right? Maybe you live with your grandma and grandpa or aunt and uncle. I think it would be so great to live with my grandparents. I'm very close to my grammie and grandpa.

The people we call family are the people we think know us better than anyone else (besides God, of course). But how much do we really know our family? Not just know *about* them, but really know them. After you check out this **Sweet Section**, I think you'll discover that you don't know as much as you think you do about the people you live with. There's *so* much more to learn. And I'm here to help you get rolling.

I'm incredibly excited about this section. Let's hurry up and get started.

First of all, please write down the first thing that comes to your mind when you read these words:

Family:

Mommy:

Daddy:

Sister:

Brother:

God:

Cam Jam: The last one, God, wasn't a trick question. God is your Heavenly Father. We are in His family. Wait, I'm getting ahead of myself. Sorry about that. We'll be talking more about this in **Sweet Section 5**. But seriously, it's important to remember that God is always with you. He is your Father. He loves you more than anyone in your earthly family ever could. (It's true!) Because He's your Father, He knows exactly what you and your family need right now. He'll take care of you today and always.

Okay—here we go.

I think you're going to really enjoy this. First of all, you're going to need your mother and father (of course not at the same time), two cool pens (different colors), a comfy place to snuggle for two, and at least thirty minutes (depending on how much fun you're having, you just might need more time).

You might not live with your mother or father and that's okay. If you would rather do this interview with your grandma, aunt, or someone else you trust, please go for it. God has placed extra-special people in your life, so you decide whom you would like to interview. If for some reason you don't have anyone in your life right now that you're comfortable doing this activity with, come back to it.

There's enough room for you to do two separate interviews. You decide who to interview first. Don't be pressed for time or try to finish this all at once. Take your time. Have fun. Oh, and make sure you use one color pen for the first interview and a different color for the second interview.

We think we know our parents well because they're our parents; we live with them and see them pretty much every single day, right? Well, after you complete these interviews, I think you'll find that there is a lot about your mom and dad (or that special someone you decided to interview) that you didn't know. So let's get started.

Use the space provided for your answers, but if you write big like I do, don't worry, just keep writing wherever you find space. You don't want to miss out on any of the cool details your parents might share with you. When you do this interview with that special someone, make sure there are no distractions and no interruptions. Imagine that you're doing a feature story on your mom and dad (or that special person in your life) and you want to get your facts straight so that those who read your special story will know the scoop firsthand.

Remember, you just might be shocked by what you're about to discover!

SO FUN! I wish I could be with you right now!

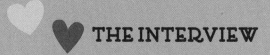 # THE INTERVIEW

Full name:

Nickname:

Date of birth:

Birthplace:

Family

What was your mother's full name?

What was your father's full name?

Do you look like your mother or father?

What was your relationship like with your parents?

What's your favorite memory of you with your mother?

What's your favorite memory of you with your father?

What did your parents do when you got in big trouble? Were you ever grounded? What did you do to get grounded?

Did you have any brothers and sisters? Names?

Of all your siblings, who were you the closest to?

Did you have any pets growing up? What were they and what were their names? Did you have a favorite pet? Why was this pet your favorite?

What about my grandparents? Tell me three things about my grandma and grandpa.

(first interview)

1.

2.

3.

(second interview)

1.

2.

3.

Did you have any family traditions? Describe your favorite family tradition. What did you do for Christmas? Did you have a real or fake Christmas tree? Did you help your parents decorate? Did your family go crazy with decorations or just a few here and there? Who did you spend Thanksgiving with? Did you dress up for Halloween every year?

Did your family ever go on a vacation? Where? Describe your favorite family vacation.

Friends

Did you have a best friend? What was her/his name? Are you still friends?

What was so special about this person that she/he was your best friend? What did she/he look like? How old were you when you met her/him?

Who is your best friend right now?

Can you tell me two reasons why this person is your best friend?

(first interview)

1.

2.

(second interview)

1.

2.

Did your friend ever hurt your feelings? What happened and what did you do?

List three things that you think are important when it comes to friendships:

(first interview)

 1.

2.

3.

(second interview)

1.

2.

3.

How Old Were You When...?

How old were you when you lost your first tooth? Did you put your tooth under your pillow for the Tooth Fairy? Did you receive a reward for losing your tooth? What was it?

(LADIES ONLY) How old were you when you shaved your legs for the very first time? Did anyone teach you how to shave your legs? Who?

How old were you when you got your driver's license? Who taught you how to drive? What did your first car look like?

How old were you when you got your first job? What was your very first job? How much money an hour did you make? Did you like this job? Why or why not?

What do I have now while I'm growing up that you did not have when you were a kid? (Examples: cell phone, computer, CDs, calculator, maybe even a color TV.)

Can you tell me three things that you remember about growing up?
(first interview)

    1.

    2.

    3.

(second interview)

    1.

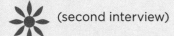   2.

    3.

Favorites

We all have favorites. So what were your favorites growing up? What are your favorite things now?

	Then	Now
Book		
Song		
Movie		
Ice cream		
Birthday gift		
Candy		
Dinner choice		
Breakfast meal		
Color		

98

Sport

_____

Holiday

_____

Season

_____

Did you have a favorite outfit that you wore a lot? Describe what it looked like.

What was the style when you were a teenager? (Clothes and hairstyle.)

Did you like to dance? What was the popular dance when you were growing up? (Hee-hee—ask them to show you the dance. I'll bet you laugh your head off.)

Did you play an instrument? What instrument? Why that instrument? Can you still play it at all?

School

Where did you go for elementary school?

Middle school?

High school?

College?

Did you ever attend clown college? (Ask this and see if they laugh—ha-ha!)

Do you remember any of your teachers? Who and why?

Can you share a memory from middle school, high school, and college? (Beware! Parents can't seem to remember too much, so if they have a hard time sharing a memory, you'll have to let them off the hook.)

How many people were in your high school graduating class?

Did you walk to school or take a bus?

Did you wear a uniform? If you did, what did it look like? Did you like it?

Favorite and least favorite subjects?

Would you say that you were a good student? Was learning easy for you or did you struggle to learn most of the time?

Were you popular in school?

Did kids ever make fun of you? What did they say? What did you do about it?

Did you ever experience bullying in school? What did you do about it?

Did you bring a lunch from home or buy your lunch? What was your favorite school lunch?

Did you play a school sport? What? What position?

Did you go to the high school prom (dance/formal)? Who did you go with and what did you wear? Did you have fun? Tell me about it.

ALERT!
This is for girls to answer only!
No boys (or daddy) allowed, please!

Who was the first boy you liked? How old were you?
What did he look like? Why did you like him?

Did you have a boyfriend? What was his name? How old
were you when you had a boyfriend for the first time? Did
your parents like the boy you liked? Why or why not?

Did your parents allow you to date? If they did, how old
were you when you started dating? (How old do I have to
be to start dating? LOL—you don't have to ask this if you
don't want to. ☺)

Did you have a celebrity crush? Who?

What do I absolutely need to know about a crush, dating, and true love?

When and where did you meet Daddy?

How old were you when you met Daddy, and how old was he?

What three qualities did you like about Daddy when you first got to know him?

1.

2.

3.

What three qualities do you like about Daddy now?

1.

2.

 3.

How did you know that Daddy was the one for you?

How did Daddy propose to you? Were you surprised? Did you cry when he proposed?

What did your wedding dress look like?

How many people were in your wedding party? What color did your bridesmaids wear?

Where did you get married and where was your wedding reception?

To what song did you dance your first dance with Daddy?

What memory of your wedding day stands out the most to you?

Did you go on a honeymoon? Where did you go and for how long? Why did you pick this place for your honeymoon? Did you have a great time?

What is your favorite memory with Daddy?

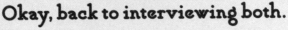

ALERT!
Okay, back to interviewing both.

Hopes and Dreams

When you were little, what did you want to be when you grew up? Why?

What did you hope your home as an adult would look like?

Did you have a dream car—a car you'd always wanted? Describe this vehicle.

Did you ever have a bad dream when you were little? What was it and what did you do about it?

Who did you used to look up to? Who was your hero and why?

While you were growing up, did you wish you could change something about the world that we live in? Why was this important to you? Is this still important to you now?

What have you never done that you would love to do?

What place would you like to visit that you've never been before?

 ## Being a Mom and Dad

Before you had children, did you ever dream about what it would be like to be a mother (or father)?

How many children did you think you would have? Did you want boys or girls or both? What names did you have picked out for your children when you were a child?

(Mommy Only Question) While I was in your belly, what did you hope for me? What was your pregnancy like? Did you get sick a lot? Did you have any weird food cravings? What?

Were you ever afraid about being a mother (or father)? What were you afraid of?

What was the first thought that came to your mind the moment I was born?

Why did you name me _____?
(Please write your name on the blank line.)

In what ways are we alike?

In what ways are you and I very different?

What three things do you pray about for me?
(first interview)

1.

2.

3.

(second interview)

1.

2.

3.

You Today—Right Now

What makes you smile?

What makes you sad?

What do you do when you're sad?

What makes you angry?

What do you do when you're angry?

What makes you laugh?

Do you ever feel alone?

What do you do when you feel all alone?

What are you afraid of?

What do you do when you're afraid?

Who do you want to talk to first when you need someone to talk to?

If you could change one thing about yourself, what would you change and why?

If you received one million dollars tomorrow, what would you do with it?

What book are you reading right now? Is it good? What do you like about it?

If someone told you that you had to leave our house immediately and you would not be able to ever return, what three things would you not leave home without?

(first interview)

1.

2.

3.

(second interview)

1.

2.

3.

What have you been praying about lately?

If God said yes right now to three requests that you have in your heart—what would you ask of Him and why?

(first interview)

1.

2.

3.

(second interview)

1.

2.

3.

What can I do to show you that I love you?

What two things would you like to do with me that we've never done before?
(first interview)

1.

2.

(second interview)

1.

2.

How can I pray for you? Please share two things that I can pray for you about.
(first interview)

1.

2.

(second interview)

   1.

   2.

Okay . . . don't forget to thank the person you just interviewed.

WAS THAT AWESOME OR WHAT?

Let's talk about this for a minute. I'm so excited for you right now!

So what did you learn? List four special things that you learned about the people you interviewed.

   1.

   2.

   3.

   4.

List two things you never expected to discover.

   1.

   2.

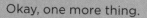

Okay, one more thing.

What question did you really want to ask your mom or dad (or that special someone)? Maybe a question that I didn't include here? Write it down and then go ask.

_____

Oh, and don't forget to include the answer.

Before you move on to the next **Sweet Section**, I really think you need to remember this: GOD chose your MOM and DAD! He did this because He is God and He never makes mistakes. You might not have a very good relationship with your parents. Maybe you have been treated badly by them. What's even worse is that maybe one of your family members hurt you physically. Or maybe you don't even know who your daddy or mommy is, maybe you've never even met them.

I can't even imagine, but I know this happens in our world. And maybe you have this book and you're reading along and you're thinking that you don't know what it's like to have a family.

STOP! Before we go any further, I need to hug you right now. Did you feel it? We will have troubles on this earth. If your troubles have to do with a broken family situation, God is there for you. He will be the parent or friend that you need right now. Oh—and He gives the best hugs!

No matter what family situation you're in, let's take some time right now to thank God. Never forget how much God loves you, my friend. He showed you love by putting you in the family you are in right now. No, your family isn't perfect, but God is and you can trust Him with everything about you. Okay?

Oh, and one more thing.

Please read this **Sweet Truth**. This verse is actually one of the Ten Commandments—which I'm sure you're probably familiar with.

Honor your father and your mother, as the LORD your God has commanded you, so that you may live long and that it may go well with you in the land the LORD your God is giving you. —Deuteronomy 5:16

No matter what, God wants us to honor our parents. I'm not even sure exactly what honor means, so I'm going to look it up really quick in the dictionary. Make sure you check it out. Respect is in the definition. I think I know what that is, but just to be sure, I'm going to look that up too. Who knew we'd be learning some vocabulary together? Hmm.

So let's pray!

Definition:
honor - verb
1 regard with great respect
• (often **be honored**) pay public respect to
• grace; privilege
2 fulfill (an obligation) or keep (an agreement)

Definition:
respect - verb
admire (someone or something)
deeply, as a result of their abilities,
qualities, or achievements
1 have due regard for the feelings,
wishes, rights, or traditions of
2 avoid harming or interfering with
3 agree to recognize and abide
by (a legal requirement)

I'll get you
started . . .

Heavenly Father,
Thank you for my family. You decided
before I was even born that You would give
me to my parents. I don't understand all of
this, but You do . . .

ONE MORE THING! Find a picture of your parents or a photo of you and the special people you chose to do the interview with. Glue or tape the picture in the cool heart frame.

ONE MORE THING! I'm laughing so hard right now because I keep saying "one more thing" multiple times. Anyway, I thought you might like to get to know my parents a little more, so Erin and I decided to interview them so we could share some of their answers with you. Check it out! But beware—our parents can be kind of unusual sometimes.

CAM CLIPS CODE: M&D INTERVIEW

5

The Family of God ...Who Are These People and Why Do They Matter to Me?

♥ ♥ ♥ ♥ ♥ ♥ ♥ ♥ ♥ ♥ ♥ ♥ ♥ ♥ ♥ ♥ ♥ ♥

You belong to another family.

Excuse me, Camryn? Yes, I know I need to explain myself, don't I?

Here it is . . .

You have probably already figured this out, or at least I hope so, that this book—yes, **HCWG#2**, the one you're holding right now—it's all about **RELATIONSHIPS**. The most important one being yours with God.

God created us to be in a relationship. First with HIM. Then He placed us in a family and put specific people in our lives called friends. You were born or adopted into a family. You already know this. You live with them. You just had a blast interviewing some of them. (At least I hope you did.) You probably look like these people in some way. You all have the same last name. I'm sure you get the point.

Well, you're also a member of another family, the Family of God. The cool, incredible thing about this family is this—it's God's family and He is the Father. God is your

Heavenly Father. His family is huge, enormous; too huge to even count. You have brothers and sisters in His family. They don't look like you, they don't live with you, and they certainly don't all have your last name. But because God is their Father too and He knew that we would need special relationships that would outlive us, He gave us the Family of God. What do I mean by "outlive"? Well, obviously, no one lives forever on this earth. Right? At some point in time we'll all say, "See ya later, world." (Well, maybe we won't say those exact words—but you get my point.) The amazing, cool thing about the Family of God is this: these people will ALWAYS be in your family. How? Well, because all the people that belong to God (His family) will be in heaven. Forever! I know, I know, it's hard to understand and imagine, but it's true.

The Church is another name for the Family of God. You thought "church" was a building with four walls, didn't you? Yeah, that place where you go on Sundays to sing, pray, and listen to your pastor preach from the Bible— that church. Well, it's also called church, but the real Church (with a capital C) is the **FAMILY of GOD**—or what the Bible calls the Body of Christ.

Listen, friend, I'm not trying to teach you Bible class or anything, because I have no clue. I'm a tween girl like you, and I'm trying to figure out this life and faith thing too. But here's what I am sure about. GOD has a plan that is

GOOD because HE is perfect and GOOD. His plan includes **RELATIONSHIPS**.

If our relationships start with HIM, then He will help us to have godly relationships with the other people He has placed in our lives. Sounds sort of simple, doesn't it? Well, of course it's not, because no one is perfect. But that's where God helps us. He helps us to be who He wants us to be in the relationships He has blessed us with.

So what do you think about all this?

Are you confused?

Do you have any questions? Seriously, send them to **www.hotchocolatewithgod.com**, and I'll find someone who can answer them!

First things first! Let's make a Family of God Tree. I'll bet you've never done this before (oh yeah!). Write down all the people that you know (NOT FAMILY MEMBERS) in the Family of God.

God

Now share at least one thing about each of these people (the tree people—ba-ha-ha!). For instance, maybe one of them has a pet frog or gorilla or whatever.

1.

2.

3.

4.

5.

Next, can you think of three people that you would like to have in the Family of God on your Family of God Tree?

1.

2.

3.

Cam we . . . I mean *can* we talk about this for a minute?

Cam Jam: We all have people in our lives that we know and love and wish they had a relationship with God. Right? Maybe there are people you know that don't even believe that God exists. This makes me so incredibly sad. God wants these people to know and love Him too—even more than we do. Maybe He wants to use you to help these people get to know Him more.

Erin: I remember when my daddy didn't know God. I prayed for him all the time. I wanted him to trust Jesus and have a relationship with Him. I even asked my daddy to pray with me about all of this and he did. Everything happens according to God's perfect timetable. There are people in all of our lives that don't know or believe in God. And the truth is—God still loves them . . . and so should we. Sharing the love of the Lord is one of the best ways to show people what God is like. So keep praying and loving the people in your life that need Jesus. And trust that God will work it all out.

Name two things that you could do to help bring the three people you listed closer to God.

1.

2.

Now, what's the one thing that's stopping you from doing the two things you listed above? Is it fear? Do you think you'll be too embarrassed?

Let's pray right now about all of this.

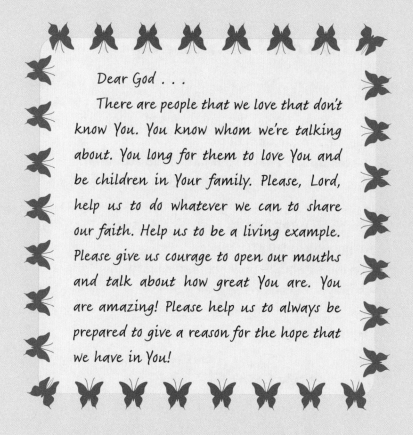

Dear God . . .

There are people that we love that don't know You. You know whom we're talking about. You long for them to love You and be children in Your family. Please, Lord, help us to do whatever we can to share our faith. Help us to be a living example. Please give us courage to open our mouths and talk about how great You are. You are amazing! Please help us to always be prepared to give a reason for the hope that we have in You!

If someone came up to you and said, "What's the Family of God?" what would you say?

Oh my, I think I have a brilliant idea. Let's ask my pastor what he would say if someone asked him that question. Better yet, let's ask a bunch of people. SO COOL! You're coming with me. Let's go!

CAM CLIPS CODE: FAMILY OF GOD

I have to ask. What did you think of the answers the people gave in the **Cam Clip**?

Listen up! Do I have your undivided attention? I'm serious. If you were with me right now I would have you look into my blue eyes while I tell you about this next set of questions. **HEAR ME!** This will be **AWESOME** if you are brave enough to **DO IT!**

Maybe we should pray about this first. Hmm. Yes—a quick prayer, because God is already listening. He already knows.

Here we go.

> Heavenly Father,
>
> We're going to need some extra courage to do this fun exercise. Please help us to be brave. It's important to get to know the people in Your family, and this is a really fun way to do just that. So please go before us as we share our lives with some people You love. Thank you. In Jesus' name.

I feel much better now, don't you?

So here's what you're going to do. You are going to

ask four different people four questions. I will give you some choices of who you can ask. You will ask all four people the same four questions.

Write each person's name and answer under each question in the space provided for you. Maybe you can use a different-colored pen for each person too. You know me—have to get the cool pen thing in there.

Listen, my friend, this is a really great opportunity for you to get to know some of these people. And just remember, we've already prayed about this, so you're good to go. God is with you. Step out in **FAITH**—and have **FUN**.

You can choose four of the following to talk to:

One of your aunts, uncles, or cousins, your best friend's mom or dad, your favorite teacher, one of the boys in your class, one of your mom's friends, one of your dad's friends, someone from your church, one of your neighbors (a friendly one, of course), a girl who is older than you.

Please feel free to let one of your parents know about this. In fact, yeah, that's a great idea. Have them help you.

Here are the four questions you will ask the four people.

THE FOUR QUESTIONS

1. Do you like peanut butter and jelly sandwiches? Favorite peanut butter? Favorite jelly?

2. If you could change ONE THING about our world, what would you change?

3. If you could bring ONE THING to heaven with you, what would you bring?

4. What's ONE THING that you are thankful for right now?

Well, how did it go? Here's the deal. If you really did this (for real—like you were brave and did it) and you want to share your answers with me at **www.hotchocolatewithgod. com**, I will post your answers on the website. I'm serious. I will. And I'll include your name. That would be very cool! So I'll be waiting to hear from you. ☺

How about you answer those four questions too? I am so curious and wish that I could hear all of your answers.

1. Do you like peanut butter and jelly sandwiches? Favorite peanut butter? Favorite jelly?

2. If you could change ONE THING about our world, what would you change?

3. If you could bring ONE THING to heaven with you, what would you bring?

4. What's ONE THING that you are thankful for right now?

Let's talk about how you fit into your bigger family.
YOU NEED TO KNOW THIS: You fit in perfectly in the Family of God.

This is great news! Maybe you feel like you don't fit in, like at school or in your circle of friends . . . or maybe even at home. This is impossible in the Family of God. You were born to fit into this Family. You were born to be somebody special—somebody made by God and for Him and His family. There's something else that's so cool that I'm practically jumping up and down as I'm typing this. Here it is: God has a specific plan for you in His family. He has given you gifts or talents on purpose so you can use them to glorify God and encourage and build up His family.

Of course not everyone has the same gifts and talents, right? We can't all be teachers (oh, by the way, I want to be a teacher when I grow up). We can't all be singers, writers, doctors, surfers, veterinarians— you get the deal.

I love how the Bible explains this using our body as an example.

Check it out!

Sweet Truth

Just as a body, though one, has many parts, but all its many parts form one body, so it is with Christ. . . . Now if the foot should say, "Because I am not a hand, I do not belong to the body," it would not for that reason stop being part of the body. And if the ear should say, "Because I am not an eye, I do not belong to the body," it would not for that reason stop being part of the body. If the whole body were an eye, where would the sense of hearing be? If the whole body were an ear, where would the sense of smell be? But in fact God has placed the parts of the body, every one of them, just as he wanted them to be.

—1 Corinthians 12:12, 15–18

I'm hysterical right now. I love God! Can you just imagine being a huge eye or ear walking around? Like, what would you wear for clothes? Who would your friends be? How does an eye hug? And what if you had to sneeze . . . watch out, everybody! I get this because God explains it clearly. We can't all be the same. He created us different, but we are *one* in His family. This is really important to understand so we don't try to be someone we're not. **BE YOURSELF!** God created you exactly how He wanted you to be.

Let's talk quickly about this idea that we're all different. I mean, we're different near and far. Our differences are things like the shape of our eyes, color of our hair, height, the way we walk, and . . . hmm. What about the way we live (different from people in jungle tribes), the things we do, the languages we speak, and the way we TALK!

The cool thing is that no matter where we're from, how we live, or how we talk—God loves us and hears the cries of our hearts. And even though we're really different, the Lord is the same. And His love for us, even with all our really cool differences, never changes. Do you know His love? I don't mean *know about* His love, I mean do you *know* His love? Do you know for sure if you are in His family with me? You can know this for sure. All you gotta do is **ACT**!

Acknowledge — that your heart aches for God's love and you need a Savior from your sin. *(Isaiah 59:2; Romans 3:23)*

Commit — your heart and life to loving Him and doing what the Bible says is right. *(Matthew 22:36–38; John 13:34–35; John 14:21–23; John 15:12–13)*

Trust — in the love of God to guide and help you as you live your life each day. *(John 3:16; Proverbs 3:5–6)*

Are you listening, girlfriend?

P.S. My mom helped me with the Scriptures for this, and honestly, I'm a young girl growing up, just like you, so I don't fully understand all of this. What I do know is this—God loves you and He has a plan for your life. His plan includes you being in His family forever. This all starts with knowing God and His Son, Jesus.

If this makes sense to you, then you're ready to say this simple prayer and give your heart to God and be part of His family:

Father in heaven, I'm sorry for the things I've done that are wrong; I confess to You that I am a sinner; forgive me. Thank You for loving me and sending Your Son, Jesus, to pay the penalty for my sin. Holy Spirit, come into my heart; Jesus, be my Lord and Savior. I give You my life. Amen!

Hey, hear me on this: *it's not about the prayer.* It's about where your heart is right now. And God already knows. If you want to be part of His family, He already knows and He has made a way for you through part of His family—His very son, Jesus. Your story is part of the greater story that is **HIS STORY**.

Oh man, I have so much to talk to you about. I can't contain it in this little book. Seriously!

So welcome to God's family, my friend and sister!

WELCOME TO THE FAMILY!!!

I'm so excited for you right now. If you prayed that prayer, go to the **HCWG** website and let me know right now, I want to keep you in my prayers. But before you do, check out this **Sweet Truth**.

Yet to all who did receive him, to those who believed in his name, he gave the right to become children of God.
—John 1:12

Oh yeah, feelin'

Seriously Sweet

about THAT truth!

Family of God

```
S  S  D  K  C  S  Y  H  P  Q  B  Y  Y  Y  B
R  P  R  E  H  T  A  F  U  S  D  O  R  C  H
X  M  I  P  H  F  S  Y  T  O  U  E  G  A  R
A  L  Q  H  P  I  D  N  B  A  V  S  Q  P  S
G  Z  Z  F  S  G  W  D  H  E  E  E  E  W  N
K  T  M  A  U  N  O  V  R  A  J  S  V  J  N
F  C  D  M  T  P  O  O  S  P  E  C  I  A  L
C  Z  N  I  Q  Y  F  I  E  M  J  P  A  M  J
O  H  F  L  Q  V  T  J  T  H  R  R  E  A  N
K  W  U  Y  Y  C  T  W  Z  A  G  W  S  Z  Q
Q  Z  F  R  G  O  D  K  Y  C  L  L  O  I  P
A  I  B  P  C  P  D  E  Q  I  K  E  P  Y  N
W  N  U  N  L  H  R  L  F  X  S  Q  R  Z  B
D  Z  I  E  R  W  D  H  V  H  R  N  U  R  D
H  R  N  W  N  X  L  N  L  T  J  S  P  G  K
```

BODY	CHURCH	FAMILY
FATHER	FOREVER	GIFTS
GOD	JESUS	PRAYER
PURPOSE	RELATIONSHIPS	SPECIAL

6

Growing Up: Becoming More Like the Girl My Father Longs for Me to Be . . .

D ijyaever (my new word for the day—but in case you need a translator who understands "Cam-speak" it means: "Did you ever"). Now, where was I before I so rudely interrupted myself? Hee-hee! Oh yeah, dijyaever . . . Sooo, dijyaever lay out on a bright beautiful day and look at the clouds? I love the way they drift through the milky-blue sky and change shapes—it almost seems like they're alive! I like to let my imagination get carried away and dream that the weird shapes are different animals, or trees, or shoes, or—ha!—cotton candy . . . You name it and I see it in the clouds.

What about you? Have you ever laid out on a sunny day and gone "cloud-dreaming?" How about "life-dreaming?" It's kinda like daydreaming with purpose, because it's when I dream about where my life is going to go, how I'm going to get there, and the kind of person I'm going to be. Hey—this calls for a few questions . . .

Do you believe that dreams really can come true?

If they can, do you think they come true by accident, by working toward them, as an answer to prayer, or . . . ALL OF THE ABOVE?

Have you ever wished upon a star or made a wish before blowing out candles on a birthday cake?

Hey, speaking of stars, did you know that God has a name for every single star in the sky? No way, come on. I know it sounds crazy but it's true. Check out the two Sweet Truths.

He determines the number of the stars and calls them each by name. Great is our Lord and mighty in power; his understanding has no limit. —Psalm 147:4–5

Lift up your eyes and look to the heavens: Who created all these?

He who brings out the starry host one by one and calls forth each of them by name. Because of his great power and mighty strength, not one of them is missing. —Isaiah 40:26

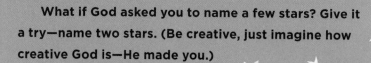

What if God asked you to name a few stars? Give it a try—name two stars. (Be creative, just imagine how creative God is—He made you.)

1.

2.

Check out this birthday cake. Five candles. These are not your average birthday wish candles, we're going to call them our hope candles (I couldn't come up with something different, so I decided hope is a very good thing). Inside these hope candles, I want you to share five things you're hoping for, praying for, talking to God about. Then get creative, girl! Color and decorate your hope cake.

Since someday you'll have to learn, who do you want to teach you how to drive? Why him/her?

If you could pick anyone in the entire world to help you with these five things, who would you pick? Remember, you can pick ANYONE.

1.   Understand the Old Testament.

2.   Learn how to dance.

3.   Help with homework.

4.   Decorate a cake.

5.   Learn how to act for a Disney TV show.

Four Things You Would Like to See Happen in Your Life . . . in the Next **Four Years**

1.

2.

3.

4.

Have you ever volunteered your time?

Cam Jam: One of the requirements at the school my sister and I attend (oh yeah, I go to the same school as my sister, Erin. Cool!) is that we do a certain number of community service hours every year. Last year I actually received an award from the president of the United States because I volunteered a lot of my time. Erin and I learned how to donate our time by watching our parents. They have dedicated their lives to the Hunter's Hope Foundation. If you'd like to know more about Hunter's Hope you can check out the website at www.huntershope.org. If you have never volunteered your time, I think you should. Ask your parents if there's a way you can help out a charity near where you live. Make sure you tell me all about it if you do it, okay?

Name one thing you'd like to do for a charity.

Two things you'd like to do when you are old enough.

1.

2.

Do you wish you could fix some of the mistakes you've made in the past?

 *Cam Jam:* We all make mistakes. No one is perfect but God. He doesn't want us to carry our mistakes around, like a backpack. After we have asked Him for forgiveness, it's time to MOVE ON. God's love for us is never ending. He always forgives.

Sweet Truth

Because of the LORD's great love we are not consumed, for his compassions never fail. They are new every morning; great is your faithfulness. —Lamentations 3:22-23

What do you think it means to live for God?

Sometimes living for God can be hard.
List three reasons why it's hard to live for God.

 1.

2.

3.

Is it still worth it? Why?

Cam Jam: Remember, anyone can be nice and treat others right—or live a godly life *when things go their way*. But when the going gets tough, are you (and me, of course) tough enough to keep a right relationship going (with His help)? A fake diamond isn't worth nearly as much as a real one, and in relationships, it's the same way—you get what you give! If a relationship is worth a lot, you're going to have to give a lot. That doesn't mean we won't blow it now and then. I mean, sometimes I get into disagreements or even arguments with people I love and say things I don't mean. But I ask God and the person I might have hurt to forgive me. That means I keep trying to do my best and trust that God will help me. I can't do it without Him!

It's all about **RELATIONSHIPS**!

After each of the following words share what your relationship is like right now.

GOD:

FAMILY:

FRIENDS:

FAMILY OF GOD:

Cam Jam: For me, that's what growing into the girl God desires for me to be is all about . . . my relationships. For one, I want to be closer to God. I really want to read His Word more and love Him more than I do right now. I hope that someday (SOON) He's the first thing I think about when I get up and the last thing on my mind at bedtime. To be honest, my mind and thoughts are all over the place. I'm just a girl trying to find out about life. And God knows me, so He'll help me to love Him more as I grow.

Revenge of Cam Jam: As far as my family is concerned, I want to be there for them more. I'd like to help my parents more, especially when they don't ask me to. I want to learn how to honor my parents more, like the way God wants me to. And I want to love my sister more too.

Return of Cam Jam: I want to be a better friend for sure. I think if I love Jesus more, this will happen. I hope that I can put other people's needs before my own. Yeah, that would be a really good change in my life.

Attack of the Cam Jam: Lastly, I need to spread my wings and get to know this other family of mine—the Family of God. Maybe I need to get involved in a youth group or something. I don't know. But I'm going to pray about it. Will you pray about it too?

By the way, are you in a youth group?

If you are, what's your youth leader's name?

If you aren't in a youth group, you should try it—seriously.

Okay, hugs! Who's the last person you hugged?

Hey, are you a hugger? Like, do you automatically hug people? (We are a hugging kind of family for sure. We hug a lot and we never leave each other without a kiss and an "I love you" too.)

Speaking of those words, who's the last person you said "I love you" to?

Write down three easy ways you can *show* your **FAMILY** you love them . . .

1.

2.

3.

Now . . . (here it comes again!) write down three not-so-easy ways you can show your **FAMILY** you love them.

1.

2.

3.

Okay, what was harder for you to do, the easy ways or the not-so-easy ways? Which do you think meant more to your family? Why?

Write down two easy ways you can show your **FRIENDS** you love them . . .

1.

2.

What about two easy ways you can show the **FAMILY OF GOD** you love them . . .

1.

2.

I think you know where I'm heading with all of this. I let you off easy and didn't ask you to think of not-so-easy ways for your friends and the Family of God. BUT—not so fast!

Now, please (notice how nice I'm being right now—I even said "please" with sugar and whatever else you like on top. I crack myself up.) Write down three ways (easy or not-so-easy) you can show God that you love Him.

1.

2.

3.

Quick question—but probably the **MOST IMPORTANT** question in this entire book—do you love God?

Do you think you love Him more than you love your family?

Do you want to love Him more?

Please STOP what you're doing and go to the very front of this book to the page where you wrote your name. Read the verse under where you wrote your name. Better yet, please write that Scripture in the big, beautiful flower.

So here's the deal, God wants us to set an example for believers (another word for the Family of God) in speech (how we talk to people), in life (um, like in how we live—which pretty much sums up everything), in love (not puppy love, my friend), in faith (what we believe), and in purity (living like He intended for us—there's more to this, but I'm only twelve so I can't really explain it all in this book . . . stick with me and I'll write about this again when I'm, like, twenty or something). I also think God wants us to set an example in all these ways to those who don't know Him yet . . . so they can see Jesus in us and want to know God.

As I said, I'm only twelve, so how can I be an example? How can I set an example in speech, life, love, faith, and purity?

How old are you right now?

How do you think you can set an example in . . .

SPEECH —

LIFE —

LOVE —

FAITH —

PURITY —

No worries, this isn't a quiz. I'm not going to check your answers, even though I wish I could. ☺

Oh my goodness—another brilliant idea from Cam. Oh yeah, party it up!

I'm in for another **Cam Clip**! Let's go and ask some peeps—some tween girls, some adults, just everybody and anybody—what they think setting an example in these areas looks like. This is going to be so interesting.

Come on, girl—go to the website and . . . watch . . . listen . . . learn . . .

CAM CLIPS CODE: BE THE EXAMPLE

Hurry—here's an **IMPORTANT** thing to do right this minute.

❃ Please find a 3x5 card immediately. On this card please write in all uppercase letters: **BE THE EXAMPLE**. Underneath this in smaller print please write: *speech, life, love, faith*, and *purity*.

❃ Of course use cool colors—decorate this with stickers and flowers or whatever else to make it YOU. When it's ready, please put this where you will see it every single day at least once . . . maybe right next to the other **Sweet Truth** reminder you already made. This is another important reminder for you! God will help you **BE THE EXAMPLE**! As you trust Him more and more each day, He will help you to grow into the girl He longs for you to be. **AWESOME**!

Hey, do you have a great recipe for hot chocolate? The more the merrier, I say. So how about you share your recipe with me at **www .hotchocolatewithgod.com**? Maybe we can post them all and try them out all winter long. YUM!

Speaking of recipes, my mom's got a GREAT recipe for hot chocolate with tons of melted marshmallows in it. Come on, I'll show you how to make it.

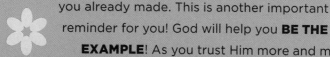 **CAM CLIPS** CODE: HOT CHOCOLATE

Growing Up Godly

```
P  Z  B  Q  D  N  E  F  W  T  F  P  K  V  C
R  D  D  T  E  X  D  A  W  O  O  P  O  J  N
B  I  B  S  A  Q  K  I  O  T  R  J  P  R  K
X  Y  O  M  H  B  S  T  H  Z  G  G  C  Q  Y
C  H  P  L  O  Q  A  H  B  E  I  Y  N  I  N
C  L  H  V  L  S  Q  S  O  U  V  P  C  H  H
E  M  N  Z  M  E  G  I  K  Q  E  Y  V  U  M
S  E  P  O  H  N  A  C  L  I  N  L  Z  Y  Q
H  C  E  E  P  S  E  R  E  N  H  S  G  Q  C
X  Z  S  J  L  Z  N  R  N  U  E  H  O  B  Y
Q  R  L  O  S  B  R  W  U  M  Z  W  K  V  C
T  P  V  A  J  K  F  P  T  T  F  I  C  E  O
R  E  B  N  E  G  I  T  J  D  U  Q  M  T  M
D  D  N  E  Y  S  X  T  G  B  E  F  G  A  G
S  X  D  R  E  A  M  S  S  K  A  C  F  Z  X
```

CHOSEN	DREAMS	EXAMPLE
FAITH	FORGIVEN	FUTURE
GROW	HOPES	LEARN
LOVED	SPEECH	UNIQUE

Until We Meet Again . . .

Ugh . . . guess what?

It's that time again. Yes, it's time for me to say "See you soon." Actually, I'll be right back; it's time for a potty break. Just kidding. Or maybe you want me to make you a homemade strawberry banana smoothie. No, I know—you want some hot chocolate with lots of teeny-tiny marshmallows and warm, fresh-out-of-the-oven chocolate chip cookies. (SO YUMMY!) That's what I want. Hold on, I'll be right back.

I'll do anything so I don't have to say good-bye.

I wish you were sitting next to me right now.

I hope that's what this has been like for you—like hanging out with me with a warm cup of delicious hot chocolate. We're getting to know each other. We're working on this thing called a *relationship* in the Family of God. We're learning. Growing. Praying.

I don't want it to end.

The good thing is, it doesn't have to.

I'm here for you. I'm only a message away.

And just so you know, I'll be praying for you.

And hopefully you'll be praying for me too.

So, one more thing before you go—like my mommy always says . . .

One day at a time . . . One prayer at a time . . . All in His time!

Okay, one more thing. We've been able to meet hundreds of girls through the website. Many have shared their **HCWG** answers with us, and it's been so fun! So don't forget to send your answers too.

Also, we're always praying about **Hot Chocolate with God**, asking God to give us creative ways in which we can encourage the "tween" scene. If you have any unique ideas you'd like to share with us—please do. We look forward to hearing from you.

Lastly . . .

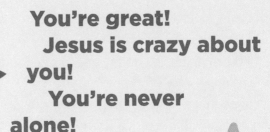

You're great!
Jesus is crazy about you!
You're never alone!

No matter what your circumstances are right now, God has a plan and super awesome purpose for your life!

YOU are the **ONLY YOU** ever created.

BBQ chips rock! (Oops—did I just throw that in there? Nice!)

Oh and . . .

BE THE EXAMPLE!

Rock on, friend!

Love and stuff,

Cam

Puzzle Solutions

Hot Chocolate with God

```
H F + + + M L + + + + + F +
+ O A + + A O + + + + R + +
+ + T I + Y F V + + + I + +
+ + + C T + M E + + E L + +
M + + I H H A + + N I + S + +
+ A R + + O C + D F + + W + +
+ U J + + + C S E + + + E + +
P + + M + + H O + + + + E + +
+ + + + A I + + L + + + T + +
N U F + P C + + + A + + T + +
G I R L S + + + + + T + R + +
+ + + + + + + + + + + E U + +
+ + + + + + + + + + + + T + +
S P I L C M A C + + + + H + +
+ + + + + + + + + + + + S + +
```

(Over, Down, Direction)
CAM CLIPS(8,14,W) CAM FAM(7,6,N)
CAM JAM(6,10,NW) FAITH(2,1,SE)
FRIENDSHIP(14,1,SW) FUN(3,10,W)
GIRLS(1,11,E) HOT CHOCOLATE(1,1,SE)
LIFE(12,4,SW) LOVE(8,1,S)
PURITY(1,8,NE) SWEET TRUTHS(13,5,S)

The Real Me Crisscross Puzzle

Across

5. Don't try to be someone you're not. Always be **yourself**.
7. Complete trust in God. **faith**
8. It's better to **trust** God than be afraid.
9. Cam's favorite color. **purple**
10. A place to write down your thoughts and feelings. **journal**
12. GOD IS ALWAYS with you. You are never **alone**!
13. Don't worry. Pray about **everything**.
14. Another word for talking to God. **prayer**

Down

1. Cam's mom likes **Christian** music.
2. You were created for a **purpose**.
3. What you should be drinking while you do this puzzle. **hot chocolate**
4. Man looks at the outward appearance but God looks at your **heart**.
6. The real you is what's on the **inside**.
9. God's **peace** will guard your heart and mind.
11. Cam's dad likes **country** music.

Family of God

```
S + + + + S + + + + + Y + + +
+ P R E H T A F + S D + R + +
+ + I + + F + + + O U E + + +
+ + + H + I + + B + V S + + +
+ + + F S G + + + E + + E + +
+ + + A + N + + R + + + + J +
+ + + M + + O O S P E C I A L
C + + I + + F I + + + P + + +
+ H + L + + + + T + R + E + +
+ + U Y + + + + A + + S + +
+ + + R G O D + Y + L + O + +
+ + + + C + + E + + + E P + +
+ + + + + H R + + + + + R + +
+ + + + + + + + + + + + U + +
+ + + + + + + + + + + + P + +
```

(Over, Down, Direction)
BODY(9,4,NE) CHURCH(1,8,SE)
FAMILY(4,5,S) FATHER(8,2,W)
FOREVER(7,8,NE) GIFTS(6,5,N)
GOD(5,11,E) JESUS(14,6,NW)
PRAYER(12,8,SW) PURPOSE(13,15,N)
RELATIONSHIPS(13,13,NW) SPECIAL(9,7,E)

Growing Up Godly

```
+  +  +  +  +  N  E  F  W  +  F  +  +  +  +
+  +  +  +  E  X  +  A  +  O  O  +  +  +  +
+  +  +  S  A  +  +  I  +  +  R  +  +  +  +
+  +  O  M  +  +  +  T  +  +  G  G  +  +  +
+  H  P  +  +  +  +  H  +  E  I  +  +  +  +
C  L  +  +  L  +  +  +  +  U  V  +  +  +  +
E  +  +  +  +  E  +  +  +  Q  E  +  +  +  +
S  E  P  O  H  +  A  +  +  I  N  +  +  +  +
H  C  E  E  P  S  E  R  +  N  +  +  +  +  +
+  +  +  +  L  +  +  R  N  U  +  +  +  +  +
+  +  +  O  +  +  +  +  U  +  +  +  +  +  +
+  +  V  +  +  +  +  +  T  +  +  +  +  +  +
+  E  +  +  +  +  +  +  +  U  +  +  +  +  +
D  +  +  +  +  +  +  +  +  +  F  +  +  +  +
+  +  D  R  E  A  M  S  +  +  +  +  +  +  +
```

(Over, Down, Direction)
CHOSEN(1,6,NE) DREAMS(3,15,E)
EXAMPLE(7,1,SW) FAITH(8,1,S)
FORGIVEN(11,1,S) FUTURE(12,14,NW)
GROW(12,4,NW) HOPES(5,8,W)
LEARN(5,6,SE) LOVED(5,10,SW)
SPEECH(6,9,W) UNIQUE(10,10,N)

DaySpring®

Your heart. God's love.

SWEET TRUTHS
FOR YOU TO SHARE!

Introducing the NEW gift line
inspired by

Hot Chocolate
With God

FEATURING:
(Hot Chocolate) Mugs, Encouragement Notes,
Journal, Pocket Tokens & Greeting Cards

Find these gifts at www.dayspring.com